ATTLEE'S GREAT CONTEMPORARIES:
THE POLITICS OF CHARACTER

Attlee's Great Contemporaries: the politics of character

continuum

Continuum
The Tower Building, 11 York Road, London SE1 7NX
15 East 26th Street, New York, NY 10010

www.continuumbooks.com

First published 2009

Copyright © 2009

British Library Cataloguing in Publication Data
A catalogue record for this book is available from the British Library.

ISBN 9780826432247

Typeset in Sabon by BookEns Ltd, Royston, Herts.
Printed and bound in Great Britain by
MPG Books Ltd, Bodmin, Cornwall

To Damian Leeson

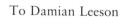

Contents

Acknowledgements

A number of people have helped me in producing this volume on Attlee. I must firstly thank Robin Baird-Smith and his colleagues at Continuum for their efforts.

Here I can give a public thanks to the superb Library at the House of Commons. My thanks also go to the Bodleian Library in Oxford for allowing me to read the Attlee letters that are housed there. Likewise I must also record thanks to Professor Trevor Burridge who pointed me in the direction of some of Attlee's reviews.

Jill Hendey has transcribed a number of drafts as well as carrying out all her work in the busy office of an MP. David Rees helped read through all of Attlee's articles reproduced here, and Patrick White's wide range of abilities have been partly on display in tracking down Attlee's essays, helping me read Attlee's letters to his brother Tom, and in seeing the manuscript through to press. My thanks go to each of these three people.

A last thank you goes to Damian Leeson who read through the book to improve its presentation. Ever since he became a friend he has carried out the function of rigorously challenging the structure of my thinking as it appears in written form. As a small recompense I dedicate this volume to him for over twenty years of rewarding friendship.

Introductory Essay:
A Social Democrat in Action

In those far-off days one could say on a public platform that the Labour Party had raised the standard of British politics, and people would spontaneously applaud.[1]

Winston Churchill once asserted that Russia was a riddle wrapped in a mystery inside an enigma. He might equally have said the same of his war time deputy, and post-war political opponent, for that is how Clement Attlee is all too commonly presented. But is Attlee truly such a riddle?

The aim of *Attlee's Great Contemporaries* is quite simply to *challenge* this image. The political classes in Britain have too limited an appreciation of Attlee's values, how he believed public life should be a living example of these values, and how this living was an essential part of bringing about the political revolution on which centre left politicians were intent. Attlee held it as a great truth that the revolution he espoused would never change the character of the British nation unless politicians led by living that kind of life themselves. The personal behaviour of politicians was, for Attlee, the outward visible sign to voters of the deepest changes politicians wished to see operating in the wider society. The failure of the political classes to offer an Attlee-style leadership has much impoverished public life in Britain, to the regret of many voters who are thereby denied a real choice at the ballot box.

Here is the first of many paradoxes we shall confront. Attlee's place in history is assured because of the legislative achievements of the Government he led. But this is only part of his record, and, as I hope this essay will show, one that is still to be evaluated fully. In an age of political celebrity, when a politician's success is so clearly dependent upon image and appearance, rather than any underlying reality, it is, ironically, in the very style of Attlee's leadership that a large part of his greatness is to be found. But, in stark contrast to much of today's politics, the outward visible signs of Attlee's leadership aimed not to obscure but, rather, to illustrate the core values of the political revolution he wished to bring about in our country.

Character is everything

Attlee, as I shall call him here for he was nothing if not formal, was elected as the Labour Party's temporary leader in 1934 and was made the leader in the following year. After serving as deputy prime minister in the 1940–1945 Churchill-led coalition government he headed, between 1945 and 1951, one of Britain's most ambitiously radical governments. Even though a record number of people voted in the 1951 election for Attlee's form of British socialism, it took, in Peter Clarke's words 'the genius of the electoral system to give the Tories, who had come a creditable second, a majority in Parliament'.[2] So Churchill, within striking distance of his seventy eighth birthday formed his first and only peace-time administration.

Attlee continued to be Labour's leader, heading his party into the 1955 election when the Conservatives, this time under Anthony Eden, increased their majority from 17 to 60 seats. Attlee, by now a full 73 years, resigned from the party leadership and his seat in the House of Commons where he had been a member since 1922. He exercised the convention for retiring prime ministers and took his seat in the House of Lords as Earl Attlee.

In retirement, Attlee worried about how he might financially provide for his beloved wife Vi whom he confidently thought he would pre-decease. (Events proved Attlee wrong; Vi died three years before he did, even though Attlee was 11 years older.) So Attlee picked up his pen to earn additional but modest amounts of money, just as he had done decades before when he was unencumbered by the party leadership.

During the following decade Attlee penned a series of studies, mainly for *The Observer*. He also wrote a number of significant essays for the *National and English Review*, four of which are included here, as well as a few pen portraits for *The Times*. The thirty essays, which appear here are invaluable in helping to establish where Attlee's true greatness lies.

The golden thread that links each of these essays is the role of character that Attlee not only highlights, but uses as a means to understand the basis of each person's success in public life. Similarly, when Attlee informs us in *The pleasure of books* of his own hinterland in his library, he is concerned with the values of those writers who gave substance to the beliefs he lived out during his own long political life. (*Essay 4*)

These miniature portraits would be valuable from anyone who had held the highest political office in the land, let alone when the actions of the author helped determine how the country would survive after the most devastating war in history. These essays become doubly invaluable as Attlee decided not to present a traditional leader-type review of current history, but to concentrate on the values held by what, in effect, constituted, at the time, much of the collective leadership of a free society.

Attlee, like the King he so much admired, was well versed in that great Victorian writer, Walter Bagehot, who wrote the classic study *The English Constitution*. Bagehot stressed how the political power of a society moved over time between the major institutions of the state and that here was one of the successes of the British form of government. Attlee's essays go behind the institutions through which political power is exercised to stress the importance of the moral character of a political leader who exercised that power, especially a leader coming from a radical tradition. *Attlee's Great Contemporaries* puts the role of character back at the centre of the political stage.

In doing so, Attlee deliberately emphasised the mighty contrast between himself and Churchill. Churchill, that great political twin with whom he was joined at the hip, left a huge, magnificent but somewhat egocentric record of the momentous times through which he lived and, in part, helped shape. Arthur Balfour, one time Tory Prime Minister, famously quipped that Churchill was writing another great book about himself, calling it this time *The World in Crisis*.

One of Churchill's many volumes was entitled *Great Contemporaries*, hence the title of this volume *Attlee's Great Contemporaries*. But unlike Churchill's studies, which are mainly about Churchill's relations with contemporary world figures, Attlee's studies are about trying to understand the collective nature of leadership in a free, and in particular, a social democratic society. Here, therefore, is a fundamental difference highlighted by the nature of the records each of these two leaders decided to leave and by which they would be judged by posterity.

Creating a death mask

Churchill's approach was nothing if not pro-active. He effectively created a whole industry to mould and cultivate how future generations would view his commanding role in the defence and destiny of the free world. But Attlee, too, was intent on shaping the death mask by which future generations would view him, although I believe much of his efforts were guided by his instinct on the role that leadership should take in a social democracy.

There is much evidence of Churchill's design, much less of Attlee's intent. But, because the image Attlee wished to preserve was, in today's terms, a non-image, centring on the role of the office rather than the individual celebrity holder of that position, it must not be assumed that Attlee was unconcerned about the judgement that would necessarily be made about him at the bar of history.

The punishment the electorate handed out to the Tories in 1945 gave Churchill the time to construct an image through which he would be remembered. *The History of the Second World War* not only made the author record sums in advances and royalties, but, by its sheer scale, Churchill also built a Maginot line of such substance around his reputation that it has yet to be circumvented. Few writers have the intellectual genius or stamina to drive through such a manoeuvre and so rebalance the war record written through Churchill's eyes. David Reynolds is a notable exception here.[3] Moreover, that literary Maginot line was constructed in the most wonderful English. Ed Murrow, the American war-time commentator, wrote that Churchill's love for his native tongue was such that, when the time came, he 'mobilised the English language and sent it into battle'.

Attlee's approach could hardly have been more different. The sparse conversational style that he had made into an art form, whereby no syllable was uttered if none was appropriate, was duly followed when it came to producing his memoirs. In contrast to Churchill's six official volumes of biography, and a series of supplementary volumes as yet incomplete, Attlee asked Kenneth Harris, an outstanding journalist on *The Observer*, to produce a single biographical volume. In addition, Attlee contributed only two short volumes of autobiography. One, *As it happened*, significantly did not carry a publication date on the edition I hold, and the other, *A Prime Minister Remembers*, attracted the rejoinder of 'not very much' by one wag after reading it. An 80 page transcript of a Granada television interview completes what was, until now, his published record.

Attlee's thirty essays produced here are therefore an important addition to these collected works. They would be of value in any circumstance. But, as we will see, they possess an additional importance. While these miniature portraits are of many of the leading people Attlee knew, they are also a study explaining how people rise to the top, or near to the top of society, by examining their personal qualities and their relationships with colleagues. Attlee presents an ethical as opposed to a mechanical explanation of what makes for effective leadership, a distinction that will be developed below (see *Making new people* below). *Essays 18* and *19* illustrate the emphasis Attlee places on the character of the politician who wields influence and sometimes, like Attlee, power itself. Anyone seeking a conventional A to Z guide about how best to clamber up the greasy pole need look elsewhere.

Let me begin by outlining those events in Attlee's life that gave him the moral compass that set the direction for the whole of his private and public being. The stage will then be set to illustrate how these determinants and outcomes of good character are what he most looked for in the people who gained entry to his miniature portrait gallery.

The values that made a life

Attlee wished his death mask to be framed by the set of values he gained at home and which he lived throughout the whole of his private and public life. That public life began in East London at the Haileybury School Boys' Club, was extended by his membership of the Stepney Council, and then continued both in the House of Commons and in the House of Lords.

Attlee's values had a distinct pedigree, combining both inheritance and choice. The inheritance was of the set of beliefs to which most professional middle-class late Victorians would have publicly subscribed. When choice was introduced, by his opting for socialism, Attlee saw his new political convictions as a means of near-universalising the set of traditional values to which he so willingly and easily subscribed.[4] Moreover, as we shall see, these traditional values determined the form of socialism that he championed.

Attlee quickly became bored with what was for him the tedium of the never-ending ritual of Sunday church observances. But this boredom with the ritual of Christianity should not be read as a repudiation of the Christian ethic itself. Christian morality remained the bedrock of Attlee's life, although the low boredom threshold which led to his disengagement from Christian ritual may also have been the root-cause of his economy of language, as well as the speedy despatch of business that was so marked a feature of his public life.

Boredom there certainly was with what Attlee described as the mumbo jumbo of Christianity. But he prefaced that brusque comment to his biographer, Kenneth Harris, with an equally curt remark: 'Believe in the ethics of Christianity'.[5] So here is another paradox. As soon as it would not cause pain or embarrassment to his parents, Attlee ceased formally to practise Christianity. Yet he became one of the most effective proponents of Christian ethics of his age. None of his political friends and acquaintances were in any doubt that Attlee's life was moulded by what Christianity represented. Nor did they doubt that Attlee lived out these values throughout his long life.

But these values were not limited to those that underpinned the evangelical tradition centring around the daily prayers and Bible readings at home which Attlee had known as a young boy. Attlee was very much the child of the upheaval that Christianity underwent during the immediate decades before his birth in 1883. And the language through which he expressed his values was very much that adopted by much of the late Victorian/Edwardian elite and middle class who similarly found themselves adrift on a sea of doubt.

A literal view of the great Bible dramas came under attack from what at first appeared to be two deadly hammer blows. The first of these blows was landed by German theologians who began questioning what had been accepted as those literal truths underpinning the great Old Testament stories.

The source of the second hammer blow came from that country house not far from London where Charles Darwin lived. Evolution not only exploded underneath the Old Testament creation texts; Darwin's work also raised a more fundamental question about whether natural selection denied God a role in the great creation chronicle.

Up until this point, Christian belief provided both an intellectual and moral underpinning to most of Britain's public institutions, and to public life more generally. As the sea of doubt generated by these two events began to lap around the foundations of our public bodies, Britain's thinking elite began to search for a means by which Christian morality, as distinct from Christian dogma, could be promoted.

One of the most intelligent, far reaching and most successful of responses to this crisis of belief came from the Oxford philosopher T H Green. His work was to influence Attlee as it did an entire generation and more of Britain's ruling elite. Green secularised the Christian ethic in a way that appealed to Attlee and to most of his contemporaries.

The acceptance of an Idealist way of looking at the world became so widespread and so commonplace that it took on the form of a public ideology through which most of our country mediated the main public issues of the day.[6] Most political figures, for example, from Asquith, who led the great reforming Liberal government from 1908 and, down to Attlee himself, were disciples of Green. Not all of them would have been conscious followers in a technical sense of practising this philosophy, but part of the success of a public ideology is to be measured by the degree to which it is adhered, often in an unconscious way. A belief in the role of a person's 'will' or responsibility in achieving our best selves, and that a person's 'will' in achieving that best self should be supported, where necessary, by collective action, however hesitantly, were the kernel of beliefs that united Idealists up and down the country.

Attlee became a typical Idealist adherent. He went up to

University College Oxford in 1901 to read modern history where, as David Howell so memorably describes, he was introduced to that great morality tale based on a faith in the soundness and superiority of British institutions.[7] Those pupils in Attlee's year who showed most promise were sent to Ernest Barker for part of their course. Barker was then not only a coming young history don, but also an avowed Idealist who stood amongst the chief intellectual proponents of English Idealism during the first half of the twentieth century.[8]

Attlee was part of the group sent to Barker, and it was he whom Attlee considered to be the most stimulating of all his teachers. Trevor Burridge recalls Attlee writing to Barker some forty years later to inform the latter that he, Attlee, still remembered his lectures, going so far as to quote a sentence Barker had used to describe the Anabaptists of Munster: 'They indulged themselves in the lusts of lascivious promiscuity.'[9] A revealing phrase to be remembered decades later by the person Churchill dubbed 'a sheep in sheep's clothing'. Writing in retirement about his love of books Attlee listed Lord David Cecil and 'my old tutor, Ernest Barker' as his favourite prose writers. (*Essay 4*)

Barker was not the only Idealist leader with whom Attlee was in contact during this formative stage of his life. After what is strangely termed a good war against poverty as a community worker in East London, Attlee applied for and secured the post of lecturer at the LSE in the social philosophy department run by Professor Urwick who was then one of the great teaching exponents of Idealism within British universities. What, then, was the specific corpus of values that his family and university gave to Attlee?

Duty, loyalty and responsibility

Christianity's influence was not confined to Attlee's adherence to its ethics, as represented by the Idealists. It marked him indelibly with a confidence so that he could attach absolute meanings to such concepts as duty, responsibility, loyalty, and courage, which are much highlighted in his miniature portraits. These four values formed the basis of the day to day decisions Attlee took both as a private individual and as a public figure. Attlee sent a sharp rebuke to a colleague who had betrayed the confidence of a royal with whom he had dinner. The colleague responded by saying that he did not understand what the Prime Minister was going on about. 'Exactly' was Attlee's succinct rejoinder.[10]

In his most affectionate portrait, of Ernest Bevin, Attlee writes 'loyalty is a great virtue in private life, and an even greater one in the stormy seas of politics – second only to courage with which it goes hand in hand'. (*Essay 20*) Attlee recognised that loyalty extended beyond the individual to those institutions who had likewise earned it. School was one such organisation to which Attlee formed an easy and abiding loyalty, and one which also began steering him into a leadership role. At the age of 13 Attlee followed his brother and closest friend, Tom, to Haileybury where he failed to thrive except in the cadet force. Here he excelled and and where loyalty and duty dug deep roots. His love and pride in his country were evident from very early in his life.

In the last essay Attlee wrote for publication, a portrait of the young Harold Macmillan, Attlee recalls that his first public demonstration of pride in his country was on display during the public celebration of Queen Victoria's Jubilee. (*Essay 30*) The first display of similar feelings by Macmillan, because he was younger, had to wait until Queen Victoria's Diamond Jubilee. Volunteering for his country in World War One was, similarly, so natural a response that there is no record of Attlee having to think, let alone debate, where his loyalty lay and where his duty began. Loyalty and duty simply propelled him to the defence of his country. Patriotism, Attlee believed, was a virtue and, moreover, 'was the emotion of every free-thinking Briton'.

This unquestioning loyalty to his country at a time of great peril had important repercussions in Attlee's subsequent political life. Francis Beckett, his most recent biographer, makes an intriguing observation. Once in the army, and promoted to the position of major, Attlee found it easy to lead men, some of whom had, on paper, qualifications that theoretically fitted them much better for the leadership role Attlee was playing. Beckett believes that this period of fighting and leadership during World War One provided Attlee with a crucial training ground in managing a team of diverse talent, where some individuals had individual talents greater than Attlee's, but whose range of talents did not always cover those relevant and vital to actual leadership.[11] It also ensured, as we will see later, that both Attlee and Churchill were able to provide a different political leadership between 1940 and 1945 to that provided by Asquith and Lloyd George during World War One (see *Affection for his political twin* later).

A Conservative Revolution

We have jumped a little ahead in the development of Attlee's beliefs. Before going to the Front, Attlee's political views were radically changed when he consciously decided to become a Socialist. It is here that we can mark the enduring quality of Attlee's values. And here is also yet another paradox, for this conversion was essentially a conservative revolution. It is also possible that, once again, Attlee's low boredom threshold may have again played its part in determining his life's course. Attlee quickly tired of his legal career which he began immediately after leaving Oxford (he was called to the bar in 1906, but had gone up to Oxford in 1901). His father was a senior partner in a highly successful solicitors' practice generating much work for barristers like Attlee. Yet Attlee took only four cases to court during his first three years at the bar.

It was at this juncture that his youngest brother Lawrence persuaded Attlee to accompany him to the boys' club that Haileybury had established in Limehouse. Attlee no doubt responded to this request, partly out of loyalty to Lawrence, and no doubt also from a loyalty to his old school; but the response was also due to his sense of duty. The Attlee family was much involved in social work activities with the poor.[12] That sense of duty did not, however, prevent Attlee from making the underground journey with Lawrence to Limehouse dressed in his legal uniform of silk top hat and tailed coat.[13] Little did Attlee know as he set out on that evening that this legal finery would soon be confined to the wardrobe.

Once in Limehouse, Attlee underwent a Pauline conversion in the views he held of the young lads who were soon to become his charge. The young workers turning up to the club were given a diet of boxing and drill, delivered through their own cadet corp. He immediately saw the importance that individuals could make to the lives of others. Cecil Nussey, by chance a fellow lawyer, was the driving force behind the club's success. Attlee was impressed by the way Nussey had devoted his life to others, and saw Nussey's success repaid in the boys' loyalty to their club.

Here was a response to which Attlee warmed, for, as we have seen, similar loyalty was for him a cardinal virtue. Attlee also began to learn that there could be no substitute for a personal involvement by those who wrote national policies, and on numerous occasions in his career he would be found emphasising the importance of politicians basing their programmes on the real needs of their constituents. The link between an MP and his constituents was an inviolable link for Attlee. The objection he makes to G D H Cole, one of Labour's outstanding intellectuals from the early 1920s, was not that Cole had a new idea every year (such a poor frequency would have offended Cole) but that Cole proposed new ideas no matter what ordinary voters thought or needed. (*Essays 18* and *24*)

As Attlee at first watched, and then became actively involved, his Victorian belief in inexorable progress came to the fore only to be decisively transformed. Nussey had shown what a difference one individual could make to the immediate lives of young people, but no matter how great Nussey's efforts, his charges remained in dead-end jobs that would see them thrown onto the industrial slagheap just as soon as their eighteenth birthday gave them an entitlement to the adult rate of pay.

The club members moreover failed to conform to the caricature that many people of Attlee's background held about them and Attlee's eyes were opened to the human potential these young people possessed. Attlee was to record his impressions of this time when, a few years later, as a young lecturer at LSE (1913), he produced a little volume entitled *The Social Worker* which formed the basis of the course he taught there. Writing in the guise of a social worker, but in reality in autobiographical terms of what had so moved him at the Haileybury Club, Attlee pictured that 'rather noisy crowd of boys on bicycles with long quiffs of hair turned over the peak of their caps, whom (the social worker) had always regarded as bounders, (but who) became human beings to him, and he appreciates their high spirits and overlooks what he would have formally have called vulgarity'.[14]

Yet the influence of these young people on Attlee went much, much further. While few people may have noticed at the time,

Attlee demonstrated an extraordinary ability to establish order and an acceptance of self-imposed discipline. Here are abilities that flowered during the 1945–51 governments. More immediately the young people changed Attlee's political views in the most fundamental way. The club members taught Attlee that their life opportunities would never be fundamentally changed if it was left to what the Idealist saw as the main spring of progress, their individual 'will', no matter how that 'will' was backed by the inspired help of individuals like Nussey and Attlee himself. How therefore was it possible, Attlee wondered, to change the life opportunities of an entire class of people?

With his father's death, Attlee became, in a modest way, financially independent. He was now free to devote his entire time to the boys at the club, and this he did. But his relationship with these young lads was far from a one way ticket. Attlee gained more than the total devotion he gave to them, outstanding though this commitment was. The club's membership changed not only Attlee's political beliefs, (he became a socialist), but his young charges also set him on the road to Downing Street as leader of a Labour Government committed to transforming their world. Moreover, when Attlee left the boys' club, his great cause, of transforming the position of the poor, remained the great moral and political objective of his life.

Advancing the poor

Placing the abolition of poverty centre stage in his political programme had the most major impact on the shape of Attlee's political life. It more than made him a socialist. Unknown to Attlee at the time, his commitment to the club and then to the East End more generally, also marked him out from other aspiring middle class parliamentary reformers. His commitment to the poor, so openly demonstrated throughout his early working life, earned him a regard in the Labour movement in a way that he could never have anticipated, and which no other aspiring middle class leader had. This appeal played a key part in the trade union support for his initial bid for the leadership of the PLP, and then for his continuance in that position.

Attlee's total commitment to the poor can be viewed in two ways; a record of organisations through which he worked after leaving the boys' club, as well as what he saw as the political role of the poor themselves. Here is another aspect of Attlee's thinking that marked him out from most other middle class parliamentarians. Likewise, his ideas on how best to counter poverty were not those of most ordinary middle class reformers. During the early campaigning days he shook a middle class audience with the cry that their best act would be to get off the backs of the poor. His 1922 election address proclaimed that 'I stand for life against wealth'.[15] And in his *The Social Worker,* Attlee criticises the traditional approach to poverty that ignored its causes. His official biographer sees this book as having 'a moral approach to (poverty) which might have come straight out of St Paul and an aesthetic one which could have come out of Ruskin'.[16] The truth, of course, is that Attlee's plea came straight from both sources. Attlee knew large parts of the New Testament by heart,[17] as he did other tracts of English literature. Similarly, in *Essay 4*, he declares that he came to the socialism of William Morris by way of Ruskin; Ruskin's broadside on the way capitalism treated the poor was one with which Attlee immediately sympathised.

This priority Attlee attached to combating poverty was one of the central driving forces of the 1945–51 Government. It is true that Attlee did little to make an analysis of his priorities easy. When questioned by Kenneth Harris on what his priority was in 1945 Attlee machine gunned his reply: 'Nationalisation first. That was the big thing – socialism: the banner of the Party for years had been public ownership, Clause 4 in the 1918 constitution'.[18]

Lord Longford, who was a Cabinet Minister under Attlee, sharply rebukes anyone liable to take this statement at its face value. Speaking on the record Longford asserted that 'Attlee didn't care a damn for nationalisation'.[19] He had duties as leader and Attlee saw a major part of any party leader's job being the promotion of the Party's policy. It is this, Kenneth Harris believes, that explains the apparent dichotomy: 'Attlee, who was not only leader of the party but the expresser of the Party's policies, had to give (nationalisation) the top priority … (yet) there is one quote in his biography in which he says "As long as the industry is being run well, it doesn't really matter whether it is nationalised or not." '[20]

Given the view he held on the role of party leader, and his natural reserve, Attlee was the last person to push his own priorities in preference to those held by the Party. But priorities there were that were very occasionally on show in interviews and, more importantly, in the programme Attlee's Government adopted. In the interview cited by Peter Hennessey, Attlee immediately follows up the Party's priorities for nationalisation with his own agenda which was the establishment of the welfare state.[21] Again, let us call Longford into court to speak. Attlee had spent all those years in Limehouse 'in what you could only call the front line (against) poverty'.[22]

I believe it impossible to overstress Attlee's passion to abolish the crippling and destructive impact that poverty arbitrarily inflicted on the lives of the families of those young lads that came to his Haileybury Boy's Club. While this great passion lay beneath the surface it was, I believe, the great driving force in Attlee's political life. Consider this clue that Attlee left for us.

Back to Peter Hennessy who cites a truly astonishing conversation Attlee had with his welfare minister Jim Griffiths when the latter was steering the great national insurance reform through the House of Commons. It illustrates just how deep Attlee's feelings were about poverty and the unjust disgrace it could inflict on decent individuals, while telling us something incredible about Attlee himself. It is not now customary for prime ministers to introduce bills, let alone to pilot individual clauses of that bill through the House of Commons, no matter how important the measure is. Griffiths was nevertheless asked by Attlee, if the minister, i.e. Griffiths, would allow the Prime Minister, i.e. Attlee, the opportunity to move the clause that would introduce a death grant.[23]

On too many occasions Attlee would have witnessed among the families of his club members, and then amongst his constituents, how hated the poor law funeral was, for it was at this point that poverty delivered its ultimate humiliation. Attlee was a fully paid up member of the Labour movement's cultural march towards respectability. For almost a century, growing in strength and pace, an ever larger proportion of the working class had willingly signed up to a distinctively working class ticket of respectability. The adoption of this moral code helped transform both the type of human being working people were and the communities in which they lived.

A good send off, as it was called, was the great public display of a lifetime successfully struggling to maintain that respect-ability. There, in the funeral cortège, and for everyone to see, was a demonstration of a successful life of respectability – or not. Attlee's wish was again to maximise what was good in life by ensuring that every working class family could hold its collective heads high as they buried family members, rather than be crippled by a pauper funeral, and the feeling of public humiliation and failure that followed. But before Attlee could become Prime Minister many things had to happen. He needed to get into the House of Commons and for Labour to form a Government it needed a programme broad and generous enough to secure the support of a wide coalition of voters. Events were occurring that encouraged Attlee to believe that a radical programme could now be an electoral asset.

The new politics

While Attlee, along with many other reformers, was critical of what was seen as the economic and social failures of nineteenth century Britain, he began to recognise, as others did, that three changes had began to take form in the latter part of the nineteenth century that placed the possibility of sweeping changes on to the political agenda. First, social investigations gave reformers a clearer picture of the dimensions of those social wrongs that cried out for justice. The great enquires into the London poor by the ship-owner Charles Booth, and by the chocolate manufacturer Seebohm Rowntree into the extent of poverty in York, were each pioneering social surveys that led to political action.

Consider the study he makes of Beatrice Webb on the centenary of her birth. (*Essay 8*) Attlee reminds us that Beatrice had worked with Charles Booth, a relative of hers, collecting data for his great study of poverty in London. But the work of Beatrice and her husband Sidney did more, in Attlee's view, than influence public opinion or, to add to, in Beatrice's dramatic description, a 'new consciousness of sin amongst (people) of intellect and property' in respect to society's disorder.[24] For Attlee, the Webbs helped create a particular Labour Movement culture, 'turning it away from the vague utopian dreams on the one hand and on the other from the arid doctrinal discussions which were a feature of some continental parties'. There is no better brief introduction to the importance of this extraordinary partnership than in this essay that Attlee penned.

Second, the social injustices that the surveys exposed were so embedded that they were seen to be beyond the capacity of the individual will to change. Although the choices individuals made were still important in shaping the types of characters they would become, individual choice alone could only prove inadequate. Forms of collective action were necessary.

Third, and perhaps most important of all, Attlee recognised that change brought about by the universalisation of the franchise had began to transform the political power of the working class, and this transformation was not limited to the exercise of the vote. The vote unlocked the door to working class representation in the House of Commons itself. The vote thereby afforded the working class more than the mere possibility of making the two established parties, Liberals and Conservatives, more receptive to working class demands. The vote also provided the opportunity for working class representatives who, in alliance with middle class reformers, could carry through these demands into Acts of Parliament.[25]

This bias in favour of working class representation and for the working class to be active agents of their own change, did much to give Attlee a natural appeal to working class MPs. Beatrice Webb, for all her great qualities, believed the working class incapable of being agents of their own change. Attlee recalls her pressing for 'a dedicated cadre of workers in the Jesuit model which would be the mainspring of the new order in society.' Attlee dismisses such talk as 'a lack of confidence in what ordinary men and women could do in a democracy'. (*Essay 8*) Attlee's belief in the legitimate role of working class MPs and, more generally, the great worth of much of working class respectability, shone through his shyness and reserve to the parliamentary selectorate and paid unsolicited dividends later in party leadership contests.

A particular kind of socialist

Attlee made his choice to become a socialist with the minimum of fuss. Only later he was to hint at the cost he had to pay in estranged relationships within his family. But, again, these emotions were expressed in an impersonal style, referring generally to families where a member embraced a radical change of views. 'Most members of the middle class who became Socialists had a pretty miserable time. You had to feel pretty strongly about your convictions to get through ... In some cases there would be real social persecution'. (*Essay 19*)

Socialism then, as now, does not come in a single package. When Attlee became a socialist there was a range of organisations bearing that name to which he could attach himself. On numerous occasions in these essays he refers to the British political tradition and the possibilities of its development in a radical direction. In his portrait of Keir Hardie, for example, we gain a hint of how a successful radical leader has to make his pitch within the rib-cage of tradition that controls the political activity of any given country. (*Essay 6*) A criterion of radical success is to stretch that rib cage and gain electoral support for its expansion.

Attlee's choice of organisation was therefore conditioned by his ethics and his growing adherence to a distinctly English radical tradition. His choice was also affected by what he read. It is impossible to say about oneself, let alone another person, whether one has a predisposition to be attracted to certain forms of literature, which then reinforce whatever stimulus helped to make such a choice in the first place. Or whether chance itself allows taste to stumble onto new grounds that then shape future choice. Attlee's niece claimed that his brother Tom played more than a walk on role in shaping his choice of reading matter.[26] What we do have from Attlee himself is the choice that he made which sets his preferences firmly in what he termed as romantic poetry.

In *The Pleasure of Books*, Attlee introduces us to this private passion. It was a passion of such intensity that he tells us that he never felt alone in the company of a book. His 'intense pleasure in poetry' was a 'ruling passion' throughout his life. The range of works that fed this feeling expanded. Attlee recalls, once up at Oxford, and with more money to spare (his father gave him an income of £200 a year), how he was 'caught up in the Romantic Movement', falling 'in love with the Pre-Raphaelites'. Swinburne and Morris joined Rossetti on his bookshelf. (*Essay 4*)

We have already seen the importance of Ruskin's work to the development of Attlee's political philosophy. 'It is through this gate that I entered the socialist fold' he tells us in *Essay 4*. Once inside, he was fed on a diet prepared by William Morris, the socialist as well as one of our 'great poets'. These works emphasised beauty, and the importance of that beauty was not simply limited to physical buildings or locations, but also in the character of individual people. We shall see shortly the importance character plays in Attlee's reform programme.

Given the Attlee Government's record, it may seem somewhat paradoxical that, in his early days, Attlee's views were distinctly tempered against a strong central state. Later we shall see that this is far from a paradox (see below *Making New People*). Yet it is important to understand that Attlee's experiences in Limehouse taught him the fundamental role the state had to play if the lives of the poor were to be transformed. But what role?

A J P Taylor describes how, up until World War One, the majority of 'sensible' English men and women, could pass through life 'and hardly notice the existence of the state, beyond the local post office and the policeman'.[27] The poor, however, had a different experience. For them, the state was all too often evident in the form of the poor law and the workhouse and, as Attlee once put it, 'everything that was drab'.[28] It was this conception of the state's role from which Attlee naturally recoiled.

The Marxist Social Democratic Federation therefore held little appeal for Attlee, whether at a theoretical or a practical level. Attlee strongly objected to the drab image the Federation promoted. Its Marxist theory also set itself against the grain of the English radical tradition with which Attlee had so firmly aligned himself. Moreover, Attlee had also seen the SDF operating locally where it had wrecked a local newspaper, *The Stepney Worker*. Musing after the Bolshevik Revolution, Attlee wondered how the wider economy would fare if the likes of Stepney SDF ever got its hands on the levers of power.[29] Again it is difficult not to conclude that his experience of the wrecking tactics of extremists at this time shaped how he responded in government. Attlee delivered a magisterial broadcast against striking dockers whom he charged as inflicting suffering on their fellow workers and their families, even though the Labour Government had transformed their pay and working conditions. The dockers went back to work shortly after the broadcast had been delivered.

Attlee, in contrast to the tight control the SDF tried to impose on its membership, allied himself firmly with the English radical tradition of dissent. His one criticism of Bevin was that he was a control freak anxious, wherever possible, to close down debate once he was on the winning side. Attlee, whose friendship with Bevin meant most to him, was critical of 'this bad side of Ernest's attitude to power ... there was no place for the rebel'. For Attlee this character trait 'ran counter to one of the most important traditions of the Labour Party' (*Essay 21*) Such a criticism had to be set in the full context of Bevin's abilities and attributes which Attlee does magnificently in his two part portrait. (*Essays 20 and 21*)

Attlee is again clear on the primary role Christianity played in ensuring that a pluralist tradition took root and, more specifically, its overwhelming influence on the nature of the British Labour movement. England in the nineteenth century was still a nation of Bible readers. He emphasised how this widespread habit, of which Attlee had been the beneficiary as a child, had two noticeable political consequences. While 'it served as an inspiration to the struggle for social justice and equality' it also at the same time, because of the variety of interpretations that may be put onto most texts, formed 'the foundation of the non-dogmatic and tolerant British approach to socialism'.[30]

The natural British tendency to dissent, Attlee maintained, prevented the formation of a rigid socialist orthodoxy, and acted as a bulwark against the rabid anti-clericalism prevalent on the continent. These forces of dissent soon made Attlee critical of the first socialist organisation he joined, the Fabian Society. His reason for this early rejection of Fabian socialism was spelt out in a reflection he made to his brother Tom after World War One. Attlee saw 'a danger in our Movement in pre-war days of taking too narrow a view – in that we can see that what appeared as the ideal life for us was the not the ideal life for everybody, with the result that our schemes made them unpalatable to the general public'. Attlee was critical of the form Fabian socialism was taking, and particularly of the guiding hands of Sidney and Beatrice Webb. 'I think we were too Webby – I am sure I was having a fatal love of statistics and neat structure of society. I think we shall have to allow for greater variety'[31]

Attlee had, in fact, moved pretty swiftly on from the Fabian Society, while remaining on good terms with the Webbs, and it was Sidney who appointed him in 1913 to an LSE lectureship in preference to Hugh Dalton. (Attlee, in turn, appointed Dalton Chancellor of the Exchequer in 1945.) Fabians, as Attlee noted, were more interested in institutions than people. Attlee believed this was the wrong way around and moved into the Independent Labour Party. It was the values promoted by the ILP that were important to Attlee. As he declares in his portrait of Keir Hardie, it was the ILP that gave the Labour Party its distinctive ethical character. (*Essay* 6) And it was this ethical code that Attlee took with him into Parliament and then, finally, into Downing Street. Once there, as we shall see, Attlee's parliamentary life was not about trimming his beliefs. Far from it. It was about trying to hold fast to them as he shaped the Government programme.

When Attlee entered the House of Commons for the first time in 1922, *The Times* dubbed him an intellectual. Attlee was 'A type that would construct a new heaven on earth on violently geometric principles'.[32] In that year, Attlee became Ramsay MacDonald's Parliamentary Private Secretary and, from this unique vantage point, Attlee became acutely aware of the change Labour politicians needed to make from simple rabble rousers to members of a political party possessing a programme that could be delivered through Parliament and Whitehall. It is therefore natural for someone as sensitive as Attlee to learn from his new position.

This period is characterised as one in which Attlee tutored himself on the machinery of Government. And it is true that he always had the clearest grasp that a political programme remained that, unless a political party was successful in an election, and that the election success was followed by a willingness to harness the Whitehall machine to deliver that programme. Hennessey observes that Attlee never lost his interest in the machinery of government.[33] Once into the war years this interest took on a new significance with Attlee standing the conventional political wisdom on its head. Running a tight ship was not important for itself; it was now seen as crucial to the delivery of the most radical of political programmes.

Here is yet another paradox. Most politicians, as well as voters, become less radical as they advance in years. Yet it was only when Attlee is in No. 10 that we see the true extent of his radicalism. Here Attlee's extraordinary personal radicalism is evident in two significant areas of policy. He was prepared to think the unthinkable over defence and foreign policy. He likewise adopted the audacious objective, which can be of no surprise to readers of these essays, of building a legislative programme with the aim of ennobling the character of the citizenry.

Turning the world upside down

On both fronts, Attlee decisively rejected playing politics by the rules of hypocrisy.[34] His views on defence and foreign affairs, for example, were deeply thought out, argued for voraciously in government, and promoted until the end of his life. Let us stay with this topic before going on to a consideration of Attlee's wish to achieve the Idealistic goal of changing the nature of the people we are.

During what proved to be the last year of the war, Attlee is shown in the official records as becoming more and more involved in overseas policy. This entry was not ideological, but was centred on the harsh economic conditions of Britain's immediate post-war position that would limit the scope of this country's power. The position that emerges, however, from the official papers is at extreme variance to the Marxist charge of 'anti-communism and anti-Sovietism that affected Attlee and Bevin ... from the earliest days of their administration'.[35] Bevin yes, perhaps, but certainly not Attlee.

Leaving aside how policy might affect a potential enemy and, indeed, how a country's defence strategy might bring into existence that very enemy, Attlee initially concerned himself with a consideration of whether Britain could afford to keep her great power role in the eastern Mediterranean and the Middle East.[36] This was the question Attlee kept centre stage. The debate then widened out so that, from the very start of his administration until he conceded defeat in January 1947, Attlee challenged in the most fundamental way what had become the unquestioned and, clearly for service chiefs and others, the unquestionable assumptions underpinning the country's defence and foreign policy.

Why did Attlee push for such a root and branch overview of policy? A number of factors came together at around the same time that increased Attlee's confidence in deciding that decisive action was desirable.

There were, first of all, the values and objectives he held throughout his life. Writing after war had been declared, but while still as leader of the opposition, Attlee declared that, while being totally committed to the war effort, the overall goal must be to establish an international body with powers greater than those of any individual state.[37] It was a fundamental mis-reading of Attlee to think he would be happy to park his ideas at the very moment he was in a position to try to make them effective. The stage was therefore set for a colossal struggle.

A second force strengthening Attlee's belief must have been his experience of how the unequal partnership with the US played out in the brutal realities of everyday politics of the war and its aftermath. Each of Attlee's studies relating to these themes has a contemporary ring about it as well as a historical perspective. One only has to read the relevant studies (*Essays 10* and *17*) and substitute Iraq for Europe to see that these issues of relative power between Allies with which Attlee battled are still all too present. When the official papers are published on New Labour will there be a similar discovery to rival those on the 1945 era, where Attlee fought what appears to have been a solitary battle in government for a root and branch review of the British Government's relationship with the United States? I doubt it.

Attlee first discusses these issues in terms of the struggle over strategy once allied forces had safely landed on mainland Europe. There had been the coalition government's experience in sharing atomic expertise when Britain, the leader in atomic knowledge, quickly becomes a supplicant to the Americans. Lastly, Attlee experienced the savage ending of the lend lease arrangements that left Britain without the resources to feed itself, let alone anything else. The position is then dramatically changed with the advent of the Marshall Plan.

Attlee's unease on the first of these issues surfaced in his review of Chester Wilmot's book which significantly is entitled the *Truth about the War*. (*Essay 3*) The concerns Attlee had about the war strategy are expressed in personal terms in his reviews of Montgomery's and Alanbrooke's books. (*Essays 10* and *17*) There will be few readers who do not feel that they have not met both Montgomery and Alanbrooke from these portraits. Attlee is aware in penning these essays, and particularly the first two, of the immediate impact such criticisms might have on the allies' wartime strategy led by General Eisenhower. By the time Attlee wrote these first portraits, Eisenhower was the President of the United States, and Attlee is conscious of how an ex premier's comments might ricochet into current Britain/American relations. Even so Attlee is pretty unequivocal, although the weighing of the issues is as subtle as ever.

War is not built on cold logic, and Attlee might have added, neither was politics. The actors, Attlee reminds us, are human beings whose natural instincts are often pulled in different directions not just by personal but also by national factors. In the first two essays (3 and 10) Attlee is clear that Montgomery had the right strategy of going quickly for a decisive knock-out blow. 'Personally I think the Montgomery plan should have been adopted ... We should have knocked out the Germans. This is ... the view of the German generals' to whom Attlee had spoken. (*Essay 10*)

But then personal and national factors come into play. Montgomery did not have the same sure touch in dealing with people of different nationalities as did Alanbrooke and Eisenhower, according to Attlee. Moreover, an American election was looming and Attlee sees how improbable it would have been in these circumstances for a British general to lead American troops in the final stages of the war.

Yet Attlee is quite clear on the gains that would have accrued from Montgomery's strategy. The war would have been concluded earlier and the political position in post-war Europe would have been substantially different.

The Alanbrooke portrait is of a different order and shines a searchlight into a little explained theatre of war – the relationship between a war-time Prime Minister and the Chief of the Imperial General Staff. He sees Alanbrooke as the right man to manage Churchill. 'It is open to doubt whether Winston would have been the success he was had Alanbrooke not been the Chief of the Imperial General Staff. Any successor would not have been able to strike the same precious balance between the Prime Minister and the military men'. What is crucial for the reader to grasp is that Attlee wishes us to understand that there were not just differences of opinion between the US and GB on strategy, 'there

was a difference between these two views and that of Winston's'.
(*Essay 17*) Not to understand this three-way pull over strategy,
Attlee believed, could lead to a misunderstanding of Churchill's
position, not to say a denigration of it.

Attlee's portrait of Alanbrooke is therefore particularly
protective of Churchill, explaining that Alanbrooke's account
could be misleading if it was not read with the knowledge of what
Churchill's objective was. America was needed to win the war
but, as Churchill and others realised only too well, there was a
correlation between the build up of US supplies of men and
equipment and the decline of Britain's standing and influence on
the war strategy. Churchill's aim was not simply to keep Britain
at the top table, but for our country to be taken seriously. (*Essay
17*)

We know that this objective largely failed, with Churchill
humiliated at Yalta by a dying Roosevelt who had fallen so far
under Stalin's spell that Russian imperialism was preferred to the
legitimate expectations that America's staunchest ally had about
the post-war world. This anti-imperialism tag was the basis of De
Gaulle's distrust of what Britain's role might be in the post war
world. (*Essay 6*) And, again, the irony is that both the United
States and France had clear imperialistic goals for themselves in
the new world order.

The fast flow of two other events must have also coloured
Attlee's attitude on how best to advance British interests in a lop-
sided alliance with America. The one-way sharing of atomic
know-how, and the brutal severing of the lend-lease arrangements, again confirmed how dismissive America could be of its
chief ally's interests and needs.

When the war began, Britain was the lead country in
understanding how atomic power could be developed for war
purposes, thanks, it has to be said, to the not insignificant
contribution of refugee scientists.[38] Once she realised the
importance of this strategy America sought a cooperative
development, a strategy to which Britain foolishly did not
respond quickly, or in a particularly generous way. Cooperation
was established later, on the basis that expertise would be pooled
and advances in knowledge shared. Any use of atomic bombs
would have to be agreed by both countries.

The first stage, that of pooling expertise, worked well. But the sharing of the technological gains did not, and there were difficulties from the very beginning. The nature of the game, so to speak, changed completely when Congress passed the McMahon Act forbidding any such exchange with anyone, including America's chief ally.

Britain saw the development of this technology as crucial to her standing as a great power after the war and likewise as applying a breakthrough role in harvesting cheap energy for home and industrial use. The unequalness of the special relationship was most graphically and publicly displayed during the Korean War by the news photograph of Attlee, ascending alone a long flight of steps, to fly to America to persuade President Truman not to use the atomic weapons which both countries had played a part in developing. So much for an agreement between two sovereign states in the use of atomic power. Kenneth Harris's interview with Dean Acheson, who was President Truman's secretary of state at the time, illustrates the power and effectiveness of Attlee as a negotiator with Truman.[39] But the unequalness of that special relationship remained.

Margaret Gowing argues that, because British scientists first understood how to make an atomic bomb, it was inevitable that, at some stage, Britain would produce her own bomb, a goal Attlee set about achieving in near secrecy, excluding most of his cabinet. His defence was that many of his colleagues would simply talk too much if they had been brought into the atomic loop. The drive towards this goal was of course reinforced by this country's feeling of betrayal of sharing its atomic know-how, only to be robbed later of the opportunity to draw equally on the gains that were being made in this frontier technology.

The feeling of 'we was robbed' in what was thought to be promised in sharing atomic know-how, and the failure to convince America of the most effective strategy of knocking Hitler out of the war, was combined with one of sheer horror as the US arbitrarily and at double quick time closed the lend-lease deal. This arrangement had come into existence in March 1941 when Britain had almost exhausted its reserves to fight on alone. Under the lend-lease arrangements the US lent or leased war supplies to her allies. By 1945, the allies, mainly Britain, had received about £220 billion worth of materials in today's prices.[40]

The lending process ended arbitrarily and without any

discussion. Truman admitted afterwards that he had not even read the document that sealed more than the fate of the lend-lease proposals themselves. Being unable to feed her population Britain was forced into a humiliating public loan from the United States Government. Attlee, himself a meticulous worker, aims a deft blow at Truman by commenting in *An American 'Statesman of the Century'* that from then on he made it a rule to read all documents before signing them, so registering the gentlest of lessons to his American ally. (*Essay 15*)

The ability of America to recover from such a serious stumble is seen in the post-war Marshall Plan that laid the economic recovery plans for Western Europe. Russia refused help although it was offered; a nasty little fact that gets in the way of the Marxist view of the post 1945 era. Even so, Attlee does not credit Marshall with the exclusive property rights to the programme that so rightly, in Attlee's view, bore his name. Attlee is ever conscious of the role that Ernie Bevin played in 'stubbornly' hanging on to Marshall's ideas. Attlee believes that Bevin's immediate and tenacious response was crucial in turning Marshall's idea into the plan that rightly took his name. It saved Western Europe from total collapse and possible domination by Communism. The Marshall plan became, in Attlee's words, one of the 'most bold, enlightened and good-natured acts in the history of nations'. (*Essay 15*)

Making new people

There is a second major area of policy where Attlee was intent not only of thinking the unthinkable, but also of trying to ensure that such lofty objectives were made a reality through government legislation. The lens through which the 1945 Government's record is now viewed significantly distorts that Government's domestic objectives. The almost total emphasis of the Government's legislative programme in nationalising not only the country's basic industries, but also welfare and health provision, produces a very partial view of what Attlee's total objectives were during the early post-war years.

Making socialists was the most audacious objective the government set itself. By considering this part of the 1945 agenda leads into what type of reformer Attlee was and how, what was once one of the great traditions within the labour movement, has ceased even to be commented upon. Attlee should be seen as an inheritor of English Idealism, of injecting the ethical basis of socialism into this tradition, and then playing his hand to its full advantage.

Peter Clarke, in his influential book *Liberals and Social Democrats*,[41] identifies four traditions of political change. Two of these traditions are important here. The first centres on those reformers who see change coming about through institutional or mechanical means. The other group of reformers see change being brought about by a moral or ethical transformation of the citizenry. Is change best and most effectively brought about by structural or institutional reform? Or is change more effectively advanced by ethical or moral regeneration? To put the question another way, is reform best delivered by a top down or a bottom up approach?

If one were to make a judgement of where this balance has been struck over the last century the literature is pretty clear: the ethical reforming tradition has been overwhelmed by institutional political activity. Indeed the record, as written since the 1960s, is so weighted in favour of institutional reform that the personal regeneration approach, if mentioned at all, is only cited so that it can be mocked and dismissed. The consequence of this distortion is that the extent of the extraordinary radicalism that under-pinned Attlee's 1945 administration is simply lost.

This one dimensional institutional reform record is at long last being challenged by the revisionist historians centring around Steven Fielding, Peter Thompson and Nick Tiratsoo.[42] This new approach affords a picture of Attlee as Prime Minister that takes him way beyond that of a successful institutional reformer, though he certainly was that also.

The great institutional reforms brought about by its nationa-lisation programme, are there, of course. But they are taken in the revisionist approach as merely the backcloth to the Attlee Government's programme of ethical or moral regeneration. Institutional reform was only half the battle, and the easier half at that. Once this fuller picture is registered the Government's objectives become truly revolutionary.

The Attlee Government moved quickly beyond its institutional reform programme, which was second to no other government, to the creation of a new kind of citizen without whom these great institutional reforms would be simply that: institutional reforms. The socialism in which the government believed was a very British affair, growing naturally from a ground tilled by British radicals over the centuries. It was also much determined by the Idealist ideas Attlee and his colleagues had imbibed in their youth and developed as they attempted to grapple with a strategy of making socialists. Ennobling the type of character possessed by the citizenry was crucial. But was such an audacious goal possible in the real world? The Labour leadership saw hopeful signs.

Had not Dunkirk, the hierarchy asked itself, not simply brought one era to an end but also signalled that the war had irreversibly altered the moral sense of the community?[43] The government emphasised, as a first move, that successful reform entailed maintaining the 'high public and social morality' of the kind that had manifested itself during the war.[44] One junior Minister who fell below this standard, John Belcher, left the Government immediately; there was none of the temporising we have come to expect of late. After the Government's Attorney General reported on Belcher's fraternising with a spiv, Attlee threw at his colleague the biggest book at the Prime Minister's disposal, a Tribunal of Inquiry. The contrast with current events could not be more marked.

While there were sins of commission in Attlee's book – the Poor Belcher – is a prime example – there are also similar sins of omission or near omission as far as Attlee was concerned. Read of his amazement that Lord Wootton first thought of his financial loss if he had to resign his business positions to join the Chamberlain Government, and that he only took up the Prime Minister's offer once his wife had sanctioned the appointment. 'What is odd is that such a thought should have occurred to Lord Wootton when so many of his fellow-countrymen were giving up not merely business appointments but life itself'. (*Essay 16*)

Apart from demanding the highest standards of behaviour from members of the Government, Attlee planned three inter-connected initiatives to nurture the type of character necessary to a successful socialist society, over and above the traditional importance radicals have always given to the role education should play in each of us achieving our best selves. It would be wrong to dismiss this programme as yet another top down institutional reform effort dressed up in the clothes of moral regeneration. Paternalism there was, for acts of parliament still had to be passed. But the acts were intended to set a framework within which the citizen would reign.

The urban environment would be rebuilt so that individuals would be able to live in community with each other. The driving force here was not just the building of new council houses to record breaking standards, but of so arranging their siting that a sense of neighbourliness and community was encouraged. In one of the last articles he penned, *Toynbee Hall Looks to the Future,* Attlee reflected explicitly, and somewhat sadly, that the failure of this objective meant that 'there is a need for the promotion of neighbourliness .... Blocks of flats are, I think, less conducive to community living'. (*Essay 26*)

Popular culture would be transformed so that the minds and aspirations of ordinary people would rise to embrace the best culture. The education minister, Ellen Wilkinson, expressed the government's aim of encouraging tastes to move from what is satisfied by today's Radio One type productions to a delight in the output of Radio Three. The establishment of the Arts Council was just one part of this programme. And the political culture would be developed to support an active democracy. That citizens needed to be active participants in their democracy had been a central cry of English Idealism. The Government placed great emphasis on building up a mass party membership. The aim to enrol most of the country into Labour Party membership was both absurd and dangerous. Yet the motive was pure enough; the wish was for people to take greater control of their lives beyond that offered every five years through a single vote at the ballot box.

This is not the place to analyse why these finest ideals, like all ideals, could only be partially achieved. But the efforts for even a partial achievement do show the extent to which Attlee was not simply the inheritor, but was also an active contributor to English Idealism, or its child, ethical socialism. Attlee saw the Labour Movement in moral terms, so when he was asked what his priorities were he did not assert education, education, education. He instead replied that what was needed in political life was 'first of all principle, secondly principle; and thirdly principle'.[45]

What makes a leader?

There is only a hint in these essays, and then obliquely, as to why Attlee gained, and then retained the Labour leadership when so many other contestants believed themselves to be so much better qualified. The portraits do, however, provide an analysis of what qualities a successful prime minister requires and are unique in that no other prime minister puts pen to paper in the way Attlee does here. But, first, how do we explain not only that Attlee became Labour leader, but that he remained there for two decades?

There are plenty of 'excuses' rolled out by his critics, all centring on his luck in being one of those few MPs who survived the 1931 election rout. But none of these explanations adequately answers why such luck endured a full 20 years, despite a number of attempts by scheming colleagues to overthrow him. The answer, I believe, lies in what Attlee wrote, not about himself of course, but about other people. But let me again set the scene.

During 1934, George Lansbury, who had been elected as the Parliamentary leader in the aftermath of the 1931 election debacle, was hospitalised for a period that required an acting leader. Attlee, who had been Lansbury's deputy, stepped into the breach. Anyone wishing to gain a clear insight into how Attlee went about his business as deputy to Lansbury, and how grateful Lansbury was, has only to turn to the study of Lansbury's by his son in law, Raymond Postgate. (*Essay 1*) Attlee evokes for us why Lansbury proved such an attractive figure to the Labour Party. He remained close to his roots, was clearly not interested in promoting himself and was, above all, driven by a great moral passion for peace. It was this very passion that also led to his downfall.

At the 1935 Labour Party conference Lansbury, a lifelong pacifist was, according to Bevin's devastating attack, parading his conscience around asking all and sundry what he should do with it. Bevin was quite clear how that question should be answered for he didn't believe the Labour Party should be led by a pacifist. Bevin's onslaught was so powerful, not to say terrible, that shortly afterwards Lansbury resigned. Attlee was immediately elected as leader and led the party into the 1935 election.

A number of academics and specialists has given currency to

the view, peddled by some of the would-be leaders themselves, that had this contest for leadership been postponed until after the General Election, with Attlee continuing as the temporary leader through the election and into the new parliament, a different leader would have been chosen. This 'what if' style of history completely ignores a couple of disobliging facts.

One can be briefly presented. No-one who has fought a general election believes a party can credibly go into that election with a temporary leader on the understanding that a different leader, unknown to the electorate, might be selected after the votes in the General Election have been counted. The other parties would have had a field day had this occurred: and rightly so.

This 'what if' approach also completely ignores the seismatic convulsions into which the Labour Party had been thrown in 1931 and this is, I believe, the decisive fact. Ramsay MacDonald's desertion, forming the National Government and then leading that Government into an election, almost wiped out Labour representation in Parliament, where the number of Labour seats fell from 287 to 52 (although not in voting terms where Labour's vote registered at 6.6 million holding up remarkably well from the 8.4 million registered two years previously). Most commentators simply fail to understand that after 1931, the Parliamentary Labour Party, the trade unions, as well as the rank and file, had had enough of leaders who, like MacDonald, placed greater emphasis on their public style over the delivery of a political programme. Attlee summarises this universal feeling in his portrait of the intellectual politician, John Strachey. Quite simply Attlee says of 'the early thirties' (we were) fed (up) to the teeth with Ramsey MacDonald'. (*Essay 24*)

Once bitten, twice shy and, in the aftermath of the 1931 catastrophe, Labour's resolve went further than a commitment never again to choose a leader in the style of MacDonald. Ernest Thirtle reflecting back to the Parliamentary Party of the 1930s, summed up the strength of this view by crying 'Oh God, make no more giants, but elevate the race'.[46] The party decided that the nature of its leadership should change. It was in this respect that Attlee, far from being a stop-gap leader, fitted the bill in almost every respect.

How did Attlee explain his leadership success? Needless to say he never broached the subject directly. The clues however are littered throughout Attlee's essays to such a degree that I cannot believe he wasn't leaving a trail for us to follow. So what do these portraits tell us of the author?

In his two portraits of George VI, he lists four of the qualities he saw in his Monarch which were also those which Attlee lived out in his own political life. (*Essays 2* and *9*) Attlee praises the King for 'a very high sense of duty'. He sees this duty as exemplified in willingly embracing the slog entailed in hard work. (*Essay 2*) The second quality of leadership Attlee gives to George VI is one of courage. Here, Attlee is not only talking of physical courage, which George VI showed in surmounting a near impossible stammer, for example, but also his moral courage. (*Essay 2*) In *The King I Knew* Attlee writes 'He was not afraid to take difficult decisions'.

Readers will have the feeling that, when Attlee holds up the mirror to his monarch, they will see not only George VI, but Attlee as well. 'A leader must have (courage) in order to make big decisions which may, even if they are the correct ones, make him look a fool, a coward, or a renegade, in the short, or even in the long term'. (*Essay 19*)

Attlee showed enormous courage along a number of political fronts, not least in the need to prevent famine in India and in occupied Germany. Despite all the deprivations of war-time, the controls and a rationing system that was regularly made more stringent as supplies became increasingly difficult to obtain, Britain had survived the war without introducing bread rationing.

Faced with a world in the early post-war period that had acute shortages of grain, Attlee agreed with America to give up 200,000 tons of British supplies and in return the Americans agreed to treat India as a special famine case. Attlee knew that this agreement favouring India and the British Zone in Germany would result in the introduction of bread rationing in Britain and he struck to this agreement despite his dislike of the German race. It is difficult to think of any other political decision over the last decade that comes anywhere near requiring the courage that Attlee showed in 1946.

The third set of qualities which Attlee believes are necessary in a successful constitutional monarch, but are likewise required of a political leader, is the ability to adapt to new conditions. The war radically transformed Britain's place in the world. Attlee writes appreciatively of how the King not only adapted the Monarch's role to these much changed conditions, but also helped the country to change. One is also tempted to think that Attlee, in moving from a traditional upper middle class household's political stance, to socialism, makes an equally dramatic adaptation to the real world. Attlee similarly praises the Monarch's judgement and his qualities of thinking outside the box. We have already seen Attlee has a surprising record on this score as well (*Turning the world upside down*).

When we move to the essays Attlee wrote more generally on leadership, we see him listing six other qualities a political leader needs to assume office and remain there for a reasonable period of time. (*Essays 18* and *19* in particular) When it comes to politics, Attlee emphasises the importance of having the guts to make the right long-term decisions. He also lists a number of other qualities that a successful prime minister needs to possess, and here Attlee could have been writing about himself, for these are all his qualities.

At the top of the list, he puts trust. A successful political leader needs to be trusted by his own side. But trust has to be reciprocal. 'Just as a man cannot be leader for long if he is not trusted, he cannot long be leader if he cannot trust'. (*Essay 18*) Attlee links character (or as Attlee once defined it, integrity) and judgement, as we have seen in his profile of Ernest Bevin. (*Essays 20* and *21*) And he links character and judgement, because 'true judgement is found … only in men of character. Judgement, indeed, presupposes character'. But judgement also comes from a leader learning from his mistakes. Judgement is therefore linked to humility. (*Essay 19*)

Attlee, himself no great orator, makes a distinction between a speech that lifts the listener towards the sky, often only momentarily, and making an impression on colleagues by speaking. Leo Amery's speech in the Norway debate was not great because of its oratory, and he was not a good speaker, but because it marked a decisive change in political loyalties, i.e. Tory backbench loss of faith in their prime minister, Neville Chamberlain. (*Essay 18*) Similarly, Halifax, no great shakes when it came to oratory either, had an impact largely because he spoke on issues about which he knew a great deal. Attlee cites his speech in the Lords on India where he supported the Labour Government's policy as an example of achieving an impact because his listeners knew 'that he would tell them the truth'. (*Essay 18*)

Next, Attlee lists having both an equitable temperament and a strong constitution if a leader is to survive. Likewise, he needs both to appreciate the importance of human nature and to understand it. The first piece of reading for each day for Attlee was significantly the birth, marriage and death column in *The Times*. Again, Attlee teases us by saying that this is a particularly important quality in analysing his own team. Likewise, a leader needs to enjoy being in politics and to be seen to be enjoying leadership.

Attlee also talks about the need to be born at the right time. His essays on Churchill and on Lady Bonham Carter's portrait of Churchill also stresses Churchill's luck that leadership in World War Two called for the two main qualities that Churchill possessed, and which prior to the war were thought, largely, to be redundant. (*Essay 29*) Attlee also contrasts Lord Samuel 'who was not so fortunate'. (*Essay 22*) Despite Lord Samuel's fine array of qualities, he was left beached without high office when the Liberal Party's electoral tide flowed out.

One last comment from Attlee on leadership which beautifully captures the basis of his own success: 'there are many men who find it impossible to believe that men lead other than by example of moral and physical courage; sympathy, self-discipline, altruism, and superior capacity for hard work.' I rest my case.

A star studded gallery

These portraits of Attlee's Great Contemporaries have been used through this essay as a form of self-portraiture. They are valuable on that score alone. But they are also a joy to read. So I end this essay by illustrating what sparkles most brightly for me in what I see as a set of literary crown jewels.

I am struck in these miniature portraits by the beauty of Attlee's language and the hints laid here of a very cultured hinterland. We see the actions of individuals placed in the circumstances in which they are taken, and not with all the gains that come from hindsight. Writing about the war Attlee observes that there is 'always the danger, when (new) information becomes available, of jobbing backwards and of passing judgment on statesmen and generals on the basis of this knowledge and not on the facts as known to the actors in the drama'. (*Essay 3*) These portraits are free of this all too easily committed error. What we have instead is judgements that are not so dependent on facts, which can change over time, but largely on observation and judgement.

At one point, Attlee calls this historical objectivity to his own defence. Writing when the debate about nuclear weapons was raging particularly strongly in the Labour Party, and when critics were reading back into the record what could only be known later, Attlee tersely observes: 'I knew nothing whatever about the genetic effects of an atomic explosion. I knew nothing about the fall-out or all the rest of what emerged after Hiroshima'. And Attlee asserts what was true for him was similarly true for President Truman, Sir Winston Churchill and Sir John Anderson, the civil servant/politician masterminding Britain's nuclear programme. (*Essay 14*)

The clarity of Attlee's judgements suggests how easy he must have found evaluating his colleagues' strengths and weakness, playing to the former and protecting the latter. The portraits also help to refocus Attlee, I believe, in a number of important respects. We see Attlee reflecting on his life as to what he considers to be the great verities and, in particular, what characteristics of his fellow human beings he most admires and advances. There is no better place to appreciate Attlee rising above the battles of his life than in his portrait of Ernest Bevin.

One of the great disappointments of Attlee's career must have been the failure we have just considered in bringing about the most radical of changes to Britain's overseas policy by advancing the establishment of a supra-national authority with the independent power to police rogue states. Here Attlee was involved in a mammoth heavyweight boxing match, of eighteen months rather than eighteen rounds, with his closest political colleague, Ernest Bevin. His sense of failure must have been very real and yet when he came to write what is his longest portrait there is no hint of, let alone a specific reference to, this Herculean struggle. Nor does his defeat affect the generosity of his comments. Attlee, reflecting his own values, centres on Bevin's disposition to great loyalty when his upbringing would have suggested a person unable to celebrate these great virtues.

These miniature portraits reinforce how Attlee saw human nature playing out in politics. We also see something of his preparedness, even late in his own life, to change his evaluations of some of his great contemporaries.

A great love

There is little sign of Attlee's mastery of language declining as the end of his life approached. One of the last portraits he wrote was one of the subtlest and most enchanting, demonstrating how good an eye Attlee had, in this instance, for both the author of the book under review, Lady Violet Bonham Carter, and her subject, Winston Churchill. Delight in observing favourably fellow human beings is not a universal human characteristic, and is even less common in individuals who are themselves the centre of attention of others. Such an eye for detail would possibly have made Attlee a great diarist as can be seen in his review of Lady Bonham Carter's *Winston Churchill As I Knew Him.* (*Essay 29*)

Attlee muses on Bonham Carter's extraordinary feat in producing her first book when she was seventy eight. Why the delay? Anyone who knew Lady Vi, and her incessant high table babble, could not but have enjoyed the bull's eye hit that followed. 'Too busy talking, perhaps' Attlee jests, before highlighting why this volume was 'quite probably a classic'. He places Bonham Carter as a writer in Winston's league, so no wonder that in her diary Lady Violet writes of the review as sheer 'nectar'.[47] Attlee's prose abilities made him a guest at this prestigious grouping, but again he fails to draw direct attention to his presence.

The classic nature of Bonham Carter's book is not found simply in the outstanding quality if its prose. It is also a work of discernment. Attlee sees the criticism she makes of Winston as being all the more powerful because the book is written in a spirit of love rather than of criticism. Winston's quirky judgements, those made during World War One that so amazed Lady Vi, are laid out for all to see. Yet Bonham Carter gets her subject right. Winston, Bonham Carter felt, belonged to another age when leaders could be both thinkers as well as men of action. That age appeared to have receded, leaving Winston stranded.

So 'spot on', Attlee believes, for an author who captures in a few sentences why World War Two so fulfilled Winston that he emerged as an architect of that great victory. Winston becomes that architect because the war called back into play a leadership that had to combine both thought and action if the war was to be pursued to a successful conclusion. Attlee was more than appreciative of being alive at the right time, and of having the talents that the hour demanded. Fortune worked in Attlee's as well as Churchill's favour. His style of leadership, as I have suggested, was exactly what the Parliamentary Party wanted after the social excesses and subsequent political betrayal by MacDonald.

In what becomes his combined portrait of Lady Bonham Carter and Churchill we see Attlee reordering the ranking a number of World War One characters have in life's Hall of Fame. Fisher, the first Sea Lord twice over, who had a reputation for instability, appears to Attlee even madder from the Bonham Carter text. Kitchener, the aloof chief of the Imperial staff until he was lost at sea in 1916, whom Attlee and most others had seen as 'a poor fellow' appears, from what Bonham Carter writes, to have been human after all. But the most significant revision of Attlee's own opinions is on a character that appears in Churchill's *Great Contemporaries*.

Bonham Carter marshals an argument to subtle effect that Attlee's view of her father, the Liberal prime minister H H Asquith, undergoes a most major revision. Asquith, charged with dithering in the conduct of the war strategy, was replaced as wartime prime minister by Lloyd George. 'I now feel from reading Lady Violet that he was in fact a decisive man. What did for him was his unreadiness to believe the worst in people' – Lloyd George was so deceitful and Winston so erratic.

This is not a criticism that could be made of Attlee himself who judged the character of his team rather better. He always had a very clear view, for example, of what Morrison was up to in his manoeuvrings for the premiership. When a colleague commented that Morrison was his own worst enemy, Bevin, quick as lightening, replied 'Not while I'm around, he ain't'. But this awareness about the weakness of his colleagues did not lead Attlee into a bunker-type mentality that so plagued Harold Wilson's premiership.

Affection for his political twin

Attlee's eye for his characters is never better revealed than when writing of the political twin to whom by history he was joined. Here we witness the huge strength of Attlee's own character. It is easier to write about someone whom the record regards as your inferior. It takes other qualities to describe, as Attlee does, of that great bay tree in whose shade he spent so much of his political career. Attlee gets Churchill so right because he writes in the same spirit as that he sees in Bonham Carter's book and, again, this makes any criticism the more telling.

Attlee sees Churchill's history as paralleling the world of battles that Winston inhabited from when, as a boy, he had moved his lead soldiers across his nursery floor. (*Essay 7*) On those rare occasions when Churchill was not writing about himself, Attlee observes, he writes only about those parts of history that interested him. *The History of the English Speaking People* was, according to Attlee, very much Churchill's history of his England.

By reminding us that Churchill is silent on the arts as well as on literature, and that there is no description of the changes in the way the mass of the people lived, Attlee gently tells us about his own great interests and passions. Could there have been a better way of pigeonholing Churchill's England than to write 'Ten pages suffice for a survey of the world events including the Renaissance, the Reformation, the Counter-Reformation, the discovery of the New World, just about as much space as Churchill devoted to Henry VIII's matrimonial adventures'. (*Essay 7*) When writing of the books that meant most to him, Attlee discloses that at university he 'fell in love with ... the Renaissance'. (*Essay 4*)

But while there is no wish to disguise Churchill's weaknesses as an historian, and to some extent as a human being, Attlee paints an incomparable portrait as this great warrior dies. (*Essay 28*) Is there an essay anywhere of this size which provides a better introduction to Churchill's greatness than that penned by Clement Attlee? 'Churchill ... was the greatest leader in war this country has ever known. Not the greatest warrior. As a strategist, he was not in the same class as Cromwell, and if he had ever commanded armies in the field I doubt if he would ever have been a Marlborough. But a war leader must be much more than a warrior, and do much more than make war. Above all, he must stand like a beacon for his country's will to win. And to give it constant voice, and to translate it into action'.

In this study, Attlee's own experience, both in fighting at the front line in the First World War, and the taking of that practical knowledge of warfare into the Cabinet, puts his observation on the conduct of the war, and the reasons for its final success, in a class of its own. He never tries to compete with Churchill by writing about the grand strategy that he, Churchill, was personally directing. Although there were politicians, such as Bob Boothby, who believed that, had Churchill confided more in Attlee, the result would have been fewer crass strategic errors.[48] A knowledge of fighting a war, a presence in the war Cabinet, together with an extraordinary ability to stand back and observe, allow Attlee to provide us with a commentary about the winning of the war that is not presented elsewhere: and with such an economy of words.

We also gain from this totally justified eulogy of Churchill, together with Attlee's other essays on the war (*Essays 3, 10 and 17* in particular) an answer to one of the most fundamental of political questions of our age: how can a total war be fought while simultaneously maintaining a democracy? Or, to put it as Attlee writes, how did politicians find it nigh impossible in Britain and in Germany to maintain control over the generals in World War One? The reverse was true in World War Two, strangely, in both Britain and Germany, but with such startlingly different outcomes.

Here the uniqueness of Attlee's style again comes to the fore. He discards a personal account emphasising his role at the centre of the war cabinet, preferring an approach focussing on the importance of having a political leadership with the experience of fighting in the previous world war. Attlee believes that the knowledge that had been gained less than 25 years previously set a relationship between the military leadership and the leading politicians that was fundamentally different a second time around. Although he talks only of Churchill's experience, Attlee's wisdom must have been valued, and not only when Churchill was away on one of his many foreign sorties. He describes in *Essay 28* Lloyd George tussling with the military but not having the battle knowledge that, for example, Churchill enjoyed, thereby failing to entice the military into questioning their own strategy. Attlee believes Churchill to be supreme as a war leader 'because he was able to solve the problem that democratic countries in total war find crucial and maybe fatal: relations between the civil and military leaders'.

The other portraiture that ranks with this study of Churchill is Attlee's evaluation of the man who was closest to him in Government and in the Labour party, Ernest Bevin. In a wonderfully laid back manner Attlee simply records 'my relationship with Ernest Bevin was the deepest of my political life. I was very fond of him and I understand that he was fond of me'.

Attlee saw the basis of Bevin's claims to greatness arising from a number of extraordinary talents. Bevin forged the trade union power base that was truly a fourth estate, and remained so right up until the point that Mrs Thatcher called it a day by bringing trade unions within the law that Parliament determined, and not to remain within a legal framework of which the trade unions themselves had sanctioned.

Again Attlee gives us insights which are absent elsewhere. If anyone was predicting at the turn of the 1900s from where the next big advance in trade union organisation would come, there would have been few backers for the prophecy that the new impetus to unity would come from 'one of the weakest, poorest and most disunited industries, transport'. That it did so was mainly due to Ernest Bevin. Bevin expressed a deep-seated hostility to Labour intellectuals, yet Attlee sees part of the extraordinary display of talents that was at Bevin's disposal as possessing an intellectual vision. *(Essay 20)*

'The creation of the Transport and General Worker's Union on a *double* basis of representation by trade and also by geographical area, though it sounds simple enough, was a brilliant idea'. In doing so Bevin created amongst a multitude of factions trust, where each knew that none would be overlooked with both trade and locality the basis of representation within the union. *(Essay 20)* Here we see how ethics also shaped action. 'For Ernest loyalty was a practical as well as a moral virtue. The huge federation he built up of smaller unions would not have lasted long if loyalty had not been its cardinal virtue'. *(Essay 20)*

It is in his portrait of Bevin that we gain a powerful insight into

Attlee's sense of security as leader in the post-1945 era. With Bevin's support, Attlee could not successfully be challenged for the premiership. Yet a number of commentators view that number 10 was within Bevin's easy grasp. That is not Attlee's view. True, he saw Bevin as the only serious contender for his position. And yet we should note Attlee's underlying confidence. He does not write that Bevin could have succeeded him, if the latter so wished, but that 'only Ernie had any real prospect' of doing so, a rather different proposition. But, as Attlee recalls here, Bevin was never mindful to make that move: 'if you go, I go with you, Clem'. *(Essay 20)*

The passion

Only twice does Attlee step aside from his role as the high priest of reserve to write passionately about himself. We know that countering poverty was his first and abiding political love. But his cultural life was likewise a great force in shaping and renewing him. It is perhaps of no little significance that Attlee did not talk about this side of himself. When he came to describe the great ocean of passion that steadily built up right through his life he preferred to remain in control through the written word. Attlee did not completely trust himself to act otherwise for this side of his nature was strong. When Attlee paid tribute in the House of Commons on the death of George VI, and even though he would have spoken from a script, those Members present saw that he was clearly and visibly moved. Attlee's portrait of the King here testifies to his feelings which gained an unexpected response. In a letter to his brother Tom, Attlee recalls that after publication Queen Mary wrote to him to say that it 'was just what a mother would like to have written about her son'.[49] On the two occasions when Attlee gives us some idea to the strength of his private passions he writes under the title *The pleasure of books*. *(Essay 4)*

It was with his books that Attlee found an intimacy that he so lacked outside his family. His love of the people he knew from his library shelves hints at how deep, not to say crippling, his shyness was. Which other prime minister, after welcoming his new back bench MPs, would conclude his address with a warning that if tomorrow those very same MPs meet their leader in the corridor, or some other such place, and he ignores them, such an action will not be because of any annoyance, let alone anger? They mustn't read anything of importance into such an occurrence for his behaviour will be due quite simply to his shyness.

Attlee sensed his political mortality by telling us that, in anticipation of being required to leave number ten in 1951, he and Vi sought out a new home. Whatever else this home needed, a primary purpose for Attlee was to house his books. To this new home Attlee safely transferred two or three thousand 'old friends and newcomers' whom 'I should hate to be without ... they are part of my life'. And it is with Attlee amongst his friends that we finally take our leave considering what those old friends and newcomers tell us about Attlee. *(Essay 4)*

They illustrate a ruling passion from the time that he could read 'and even before, I have had an intense pleasure in poetry'. The death in October 1892 of Tennyson is for Attlee a personal blow for, as a nine year old, his hero appeared immortal. At Haileybury, he was introduced to Browning, gained a good knowledge of Shakespeare and then, at Oxford, added Swinburne and Morris and Rossetti. The choice of poets reveals much about a person. A ministerial colleague, Lord Salter, has written about 'a Mongolian impassivity in (Attlee's) facial expression'.[50] Yet behind this facial expression bubbled a character that was naturally drawn to the romantic poets.

In a Library Association lecture, Attlee remarkably reports 'I'm never alone, even if I have no books' and the reason for this was Attlee's extraordinary memory. 'I can call upon abundant stories from memory. I recall how, in World War One, I used to spend the long nights keeping awake in Gallipoli or France and I would set myself the task of repeating to myself a hundred lines from so many poets or so many writers'.[51]

Attlee also saw his treasury of memories as a means both of helping to understand as well as to revive his spirits. In 1940, the lowest point in the war from a British perspective, Attlee 'wanted a little refreshment'. In a passage like no other Attlee illustrates what an extraordinary self-contained individual he was. The library beckoned and there 'I re-read a great speech of Pericles on the dead at Marathon'. Attlee wanted to be reminded that other people had been in as difficult a position as Britain then found itself. 'And one recalls that just as Athens stood against the barbarians of Persia, so we were standing for civilization against the Nazis'.[52]

Affirming old friends, and meeting new ones, was clearly an essential part of Attlee's hinterland. Not many prime ministers during the last century, apart from Macmillan, perhaps, would, like Attlee, have so ordered his day that, while at Chequers, he read Gibbon right through. Nor would many previous premiers have written about those books and the associated memories that were cherished. For it was on his book shelves that Attlee stored many memories. His books on Gallipoli, which had been joined by those from his brother's collection when the latter died, and to which he reverts quite often, not merely to reweigh the strategy but to recall 'the lads with whom I trained in 1914, so many of whom lie there in the Peninsula'.

And there, on that peninsula, we leave Attlee. Just as Attlee treasured the memories of his fallen comrades in arms, so too should a democracy valuing its freedom remember the type of leadership provided by a man who was far from being labelled the riddle that so many post-war commentators have tied to him.

References

1 Douglas Jay, in *Attlee As I Knew Him*, ed. Geoffrey Dellar, London Borough of Tower Hamlets, 1983, 25.
2 Peter Clarke, 'Attlee: the making of the post-war consensus' in *A Question of Leadership*, Penguin Books, 1991, 198.
3 David Reynolds, *In Command of History*, Allen Lane, 2004.
4 Trevor Burridge, *Clement Attlee*, Cape, 1985, 20.
5 Kenneth Harris, *Attlee*, Weidenfeld and Nicolson, 1995, 564.
6 Jose Harris, 'Political Thought and the Welfare State 1870–1940', *Past and Present*, 135, 1992.
7 David Howell, *Attlee*, Haus Publishing, 2006, 5.
8 Julia Stapleton, *Englishness and the Study of Politics*, Cambridge, 1994.
9 Burridge, 18.
10 Woodrow Wyatt, in *Attlee as I knew him*, 47.
11 Francis Becklett, *Clem Attlee*, Richard Cohen Books, 1997, 45–57.
12 Peggy Attlee, *With a quiet conscience: a biography of Thomas Simons Attlee*, Dove and Clough Press, 1995, 30.

13 Burridge, 10.
14 Cited in R. C. Whiting, 'Clement Richard Attlee' *Oxford Dictionary of National biography*, Oxford, 2004, 875.
15 Harris, 55.
16 Harris, 49.
17 Kenneth Harris cites his sister Mary, in *Attlee*, 5.
18 Peter Hennessy, *Muddling Through*, Gollance, 1996, 172.
19 Harris, 172.
20 Harris, 48–9.
21 Hennessy, 173.
22 Hennessy, 172.
23 Hennessy, 174.
24 Beatrice Webb, *My Apprenticeship*, Longman, 1942, 154.
25 W. Golant, 'The early political though of C. R. Attlee' *Political Quarterly*, 40 (1969), 249.
26 Peggy Attlee, 30.
27 A. J. P. Taylor, *English History 1914–1945*, Penguin, 1975, 1.
28 Burridge, 29.
29 W. Golant, 'The early political thought of C. R. Attlee', *Political Quarterly*, 40, 248.
30 C. R. Attlee, *The Labour Party in Perspective*, Gollance, 1937, 27.
31 Quoted in W. Golant, 'The early political thought of C. R. Attlee, 247.
32 Golant, 'The early political thought of C. R. Attlee', 247.
33 Hennessy, *The Prime Minister*, Allen Lane, 2000, chapter 7.
34 David Runciman, *Political Hypocrisy*, University Presses of California, Columbia and Princetown, 2008.
35 John Saville, 'C. R. Attlee: An Assessment', in *Socialist Register*, Merlin Press, 1983, 157.
36 Raymond Smith and John Zametica, 'The Cold Warrior: Clement Attlee reconsidered, 1945–7', *International Affairs*, Spring, 1985.
37 Smith and Zametica, 239.
38 Margaret Gowing, 'Britain, America and the Bomb', in *Retreat from Power*, ed David Dilkes, Macmillan, 1981.
39 *The Listener*, 8 April 1971, 442.
40 House of Commons Library, 12 November 2008.
41 CUP, 1978.
42 '*England Arise!' The Labour Party and popular politics in 1940's Britain*, Manchester University Press, 1995.

43 *England Arise*, 81.

44 *England Arise*, 82.

45 Quoted in Golant, 'The Early Political Thought', 255.

46 E. Thirtle, *Time's Winged Chariot*, Chaterson, 1945, 125.

47 *Daring to hope, the diaries and letters of Violet Bonham Carter 1946–1969*, ed Mark Pottle, Weidenfeld and Nicholson, 2000, 301.

48 Lord Boothby, in *Attlee as I knew him*, 17.

49 Letter dated 18 February 1952 in the Bodleian Library, GB, MSS, Eng.c 4791-4.

50 Lord Salter, *Memoirs of a public servant*, Faber & Faber, 1961, 285.

51 *The Library Association Record*, 281.

52 *The Library Association Record*, 281.

1

Lansbury of London

In his Life of George Lansbury, Mr. Raymond Postgate has done an admirable piece of work and has put all of us who loved and worked with 'G. L.' under a debt of gratitude. While the book is informed throughout with love and admiration for its subject, it is nevertheless written with real discrimination. Mr. Postgate has, very wisely, given a clear picture of the time when George Lansbury started his career and of the conditions that then obtained in East London. He has also dealt with the period before the 1914 war in considerable detail. To people of my generation this is still modern times. I was myself a rank-and-file member of the Socialist movement during those years, but to the younger generation this is now ancient history and the struggles of that time are apt to be disregarded.

George Lansbury was a Victorian. He grew up at a time when to the members of the ruling classes the world seemed to be progressing steadily and the existing state of society to be stable and satisfactory. But the Victorian age, if it produced a complacent majority, was also rich in leaders of revolt, and of these George Lansbury was by no means the least.

***

It would have been easy for Lansbury to have remained in the Liberal Party. He was an able businessman with a large family dependent upon him. He might have quieted his social conscience by taking part in charitable work and advocating mild social reforms, but he was possessed by a burning passion for social justice and a deep compassion for suffering. He became one of the foremost agitators of his time, but also – and this is important – a practical administrator.

1

This is well exemplified in his attack on the old Poor Law system. The Webbs in their famous Minority Report destroyed the arguments for it, but it was Lansbury and Crooks who, by their much-abused Poplarism, really dealt the death-blow to the old system. Poplarism was regarded as the indiscriminate handing out of public money to all and sundry, but Mr. Postgate shows how unjust this charge was. Lansbury in Poplar was a wise and careful administrator and his attitude on the Means Test shows how far he was from being a mere woolly sentimentalist.

It was not the least of Mr. MacDonald's mistakes that he failed to utilise Lansbury's great abilities. This, no doubt, was due to a complete incompatibility of temperament. Lansbury was noisy and tempestuous. He was out to get things done and this did not suit MacDonald. He was once described by the 'Morning Post' as that 'rampageous old socialist' and the epithet had some justification, but the idea that Lansbury was all heart and no head was, as Mr. Postgate shows, entirely erroneous.

***

I worked very closely with Lansbury when he led the small Labour Party in the 1931 Parliament and learnt to have a great respect for his judgment. I recall a leading Conservative saying to a Labour Member who had said, 'I think George Lansbury is the best man I have ever known.' 'Best, is that all? He's the ablest Leader of an Opposition that I've ever seen.' This was true. Mr. Baldwin once said that the little band of Labour men had saved Parliamentary institutions. This was largely due to Lansbury's leadership. One great source of strength which he had was his power to inspire affection, not only in those who were his immediate colleagues, but in thousands of men and women throughout the country 'Good old George' reflected real feeling.

Another source of strength was his firmly held Christian faith. A convinced Anglican, he was nevertheless ready to work with men of all creeds or of none at all, for he was quite free from intolerance and pharisaism. He was always ready to respect the convictions of others. This was so even where the division was most deep as in his attitude to war. He understood that other people who could not accept his views were none the less sincere. Such toleration is not always found among pacifists.

On the question of war he was, I think, irrational. Here, if anywhere, his heart ruled his head. He seemed to believe that other people must see the thing as he did if only the matter was put fully before them. Hence his last pathetic pilgrimage round the world in the belief that even Hitler could be persuaded by sweet reasonableness of the evil of his ways.

Mr. Postgate does not attempt to gloss over the mistakes which Lansbury made in his career; mistakes which later in his life, as in the instance of his resignation of his seat to fight as a Women's Suffrage candidate, he freely admitted, but when these errors are taken into account they weigh very lightly in the scales against the magnitude of his achievements, for these are not confined to those accomplished in his own lifetime. He and others sowed the seed of the harvest which was reaped in the years after the Second World War. It was Lansbury and the men and women of his generation who did so much to change the climate of opinion in this country.

***

The social doctrines that Lansbury and others were proclaiming forty or fifty years ago have in so many instances now become the assumptions which are to-day generally accepted.

Mr. Postgate has done well to bring out how very English Lansbury was and how great was his love of England. His sympathies were worldwide, but they were based on his love of his native land and of its people. That cheerful figure with the side-whiskers and the bowler hat, greeting all and sundry as 'Brother,' could only have been bred in England, and as a loyal cockney I would say could only have become the man he was in London.

The East End with its lights and shadows is passing away, a new Poplar and a new Stepney are being born, part of which bears his name. I hope that the young men and women who will have the duty of carrying on his work will read, mark and learn this life of George Lansbury.

The Life of George Lansbury by Raymond Postgate.
Longmans, 1951

2
The King I Knew

The death of King George the Sixth came as a great shock to all his people. I think that everyone to a greater or lesser degree felt a sense of personal loss. To me this feeling was very real. I had had the privilege of serving him as a Minister for eleven years, during the last six years of which I was Prime Minister. During this latter period there was seldom a week in which I did not see him to discuss affairs of State. The longer I served him the greater was my admiration, respect and affection. No Prime Minister had a kinder or more considerate master.

In the long roll of British Monarchs he will deservedly take a high place.

The functions of Kingship have changed during the centuries from the times when Kings not only reigned but ruled, but it would be a mistake to think that constitutional monarchy does not demand high qualities from the occupant of the Throne. On the contrary, the constitutional head of a democracy has an exacting task. He needs to have a broad and sympathetic appreciation of the feelings of the people, for he is in a special sense their representative.

Many Peoples

This is so even in a small and homogeneous State, but it is still more important where the King reigns over many peoples. King George was King not only of the people of these islands but of many other nations – some fully self-governing, others at various stages on the way thereto. It is also an exacting task to be King in times of change, when new forces are coming to the front. The Monarch needs to be broadminded and receptive to new ideas.

King George was, I think, fortunate in not being born to succeed to the throne. His earlier life was not shadowed by the knowledge of heavy responsibilities to come. He was able to live a life more like that of his future subjects. He served as an officer in the Navy during the First World War. Subsequently he was interested in industrial welfare and in boys' camps, and he acquired a wider knowledge of industrial conditions and social and economic questions than is usual in a member of a Royal House. He was happily married and could enjoy family life without the heavy responsibilities that fall upon a King.

King George was called to the Throne in circumstances that must have caused him distress. It is a tribute to him and to Her Gracious Majesty the Queen Mother that they so soon established themselves firmly in the hearts of the people.

Duty First

King George had in a high degree the qualities which are required in a constitutional Monarch. I think that I would put first his great sense of duty. He regarded himself as the servant of his people, and duty always came first. Few people perhaps realised how hard he worked. They knew that he had public duties to perform. They probably understood that there were many formalities to be observed, but they did not know the close attention which he gave to every side of public affairs. Masses of telegrams, reports and other State papers came before him and he never treated them perfunctorily.

I was always careful to be up to date in my reading whenever I went to see him, for I knew that he would be well informed on everything, whether foreign or domestic. He often told me how surprised visiting statesmen were at the extent of his knowledge. 'They don't seem to realise I have to work,' he would say. I knew, too, that I would always get from him a well-balanced judgment.

Complete Calm

It is one of the privileges of a Prime Minister to be able to discuss affairs of State with a man who is above the political battle, and who has had a long and continuous experience both of things and persons.

I think I would put next his courage. Physical courage, of course, he had to the full, as he showed in two wars, and most notably when he was stricken with illness. He faced the danger of an operation with complete calm. But he also had moral courage. He was not afraid to take difficult decisions. Throughout his life he was sustained by his strong religious faith.

King George had great personal charm. He had a ready sense of humour and was a delightful host. I always admired the way he would put his guests at ease. He never in any way derogated from dignity, but at the same time he freed one from any feeling of awkwardness or constraint.

He was broadminded and tolerant. It cannot, I think, have been easy for him to have had a Government returned to power with a majority pledged to make sweeping changes, but he accepted the position. I never knew him to depart from strict constitutional propriety. He had studied economic and social questions, and whether or not he agreed with the policy of the Labour Government, he understood very well the reasons for it.

A Long Strain

He showed the same broadmindedness in dealing with the problems of the Commonwealth. Here again, he realised that changes were inevitable, and with sure judgment he discerned between essentials and non-essentials.

King George did not reign in tranquil times. The earlier part of his reign was overshadowed by the growing menace of Hitlerism and the increasing possibility of war. Then came the long strain of the war, and, in his later years, the tensions and stresses of the period in which we live.

I think that this continual anxiety weighed upon him. He was deeply solicitous for his people's welfare. He earnestly desired peace, but looking round the world situation he saw all too few bright spots and far too many clouds on the horizon. He had, on the other hand, a happy family life, and he knew how great was the affection in which he was held by his peoples throughout the Commonwealth and Empire.

Death has taken him from us, but I believe that his devotion to duty will continue for many years to inspire his people. I know the hearts of all feel deep sympathy for the Royal Family in their great loss, and offer fervent good wishes to our Gracious Queen Elizabeth the Second.

3

Truth About the War

In *The Struggle for Europe** Mr. Chester Wilmot has made a
contribution of first-class importance to the history of the Second
World War. This alone would entitle the book to receive the
careful attention of all serious students of public affairs.

But he has done more than this. He has posed two major
questions of strategy, the one political and the other military. The
actual decisions which he reviews were momentous, not only for
winning the war, but for deciding what kind of a world would
emerge when peace returned. The book is well written and is an
admirable description of the contest: it is also well supplied with
maps. We have already Mr. Churchill's great work and General
Eisenhower's *Crusade in Europe*. We have the despatches of Lord
Montgomery and Lord Alexander and many other books on the
War. But here we have the struggle viewed from both sides. Mr.
Wilmot has had access to a mass of information derived from
documents and from personal testimony on what was happening
'on the other side of the hill.' This gives the book unique value.

There is, of course, always the danger, when information of
this kind becomes available, of jobbing backwards and of passing
judgment on statesmen and generals on the basis of this
knowledge and not of the facts as known to the actors in the
drama. Mr. Wilmot has not fallen into this error. The possession
of this information, on the other hand, is of the greatest value in
enabling us to appreciate the risks taken in particular operations.
To give an example: when it was decided to land in Normandy, I
always had the fear that we might be held at the beaches or

The Struggle for Europe by Chester Wilmot, Collins, 1952.

bogged down in some narrow perimeter. This was a natural apprehension by one who had served in Gallipoli. It might well have happened again. Mr. Wilmot shows from German sources how completely the Germans were deceived by our cover plan. It was weeks before they realized that Normandy, not the Pas de Calais, was the venue for the major invasion of Europe. Powerful forces were retained in the North when they might have turned the scale in Normandy. Our air interdiction was a great factor in the success of the operation, but German failure to appreciate the situation was of even greater importance.

Mr. Wilmot's narrative is eminently readable and contains passages which are intensely dramatic. I liked particularly his description of the tense hours during which weather reports kept coming in prior to General Eisenhower's brave decision to go ahead with the invasion of France. Again the episode of the landing of the paratroops in Normandy is described by one who was, as a war correspondent, actually present. These are highlights: but the author is no less successful in his description of other events. Throughout we have the picture of what was happening on the German side. We see Hitler, disregarding the advice of his generals, bringing off dramatic successes in the early stages of the War, and we see how those successes enabled him to take the control of military operations out of the hands of his skilled advisers and indeed, in the later stages, actually to interfere in the details of operations in the field. Such was his prestige that experienced soldiers had to do things which all their training taught them were wrong. In the end we see the 'inspired corporal' leaving himself without adequate forces at the crucial points through his wide dispersion of forces and his fanatical refusal to give ground anywhere. Throughout one sees the interplay of military and political considerations. The criticism of the Germans in the First World War was that the military were given a free hand while the politicians lost all control over events. In the Second World War the reverse happened. It was indeed fortunate for the Allies that this was so, for had there been proper co-operation between the military and the political elements the Germans would have had a big advantage.

For the book brings out very clearly the difficulties that beset allies in war. Nothing is harder than to get concerted action between allies whose estimates of the importance of political objectives differ, whose strategic traditions vary and whose national susceptibilities have to be met. This brings me to the first of the two major questions which are discussed in this book. What was the correct political strategy for the Allies? From the point of view of the Russians, the one immediate aim was to beat off the attack on their own country and to get as much of the weight as possible taken off them by the Western Powers. Discussion of further objectives would come later. President Roosevelt had seen from the first the danger to America of German hegemony in Europe, and he did his utmost to prepare his countrymen for entry into the War: but the decisive factor was the attack on Pearl Harbour.

It is to the great credit of the American leaders, civil and military, that despite this they recognized that the decisive arena was Europe. This was the vital decision taken at the Arcadia Conference. While the Japanese had to be held in the East, the first major blow must be struck in the West. I recall General Marshall coming over to expound his plans for an American attack on Europe in 1942. I remember how we welcomed this decision, though we knew that the expedition could not possibly be staged so soon. At that time the Americans failed to appreciate the immense amount of work required before such an operation could be undertaken with any hope of success. It was unfortunate that the Russians, who had no understanding of what an amphibious operation on a large scale entailed, were led to expect an early opening of a Second Front. This misconception led to much friction with our Allies. It led also to an unwillingness on the part of the Americans to undertake operations such as, for instance, those in the Mediterranean, which seemed to them irrelevant and a diversion of forces from the main objective.

In fact, quite apart from the question as to whether a direct attack on the West or an indirect attack on what Mr. Churchill called the 'soft underbelly of the Axis' was the right strategy, the Mediterranean offered the only opportunity for effective action by land forces at this stage of the War. I think that the President had a truer appreciation of the importance of the Mediterranean than had his service advisers, for I remember, when I discussed Allied strategy with him two months before Pearl Harbour, he pointed to Algiers on the map and said, 'That is where I want to see American troops.' In the event American forces did land in

North Africa, the very real menace to the Middle East was removed by El Alamein, and Africa was cleansed of Fascists. The question then arose: 'What next?' It took much persuasion to convince the Americans that it was right to continue the operation so as to knock the Duce out of the War. They were reluctant to divert forces, and especially transport, from the main theatre – the West. Mr. Wilmot shows clearly that here was a clash of opinion in the field of political as well as military strategy. Our traditional policy as a naval Power with only small land forces has been to make full use of the mobility bestowed by sea power. We remember how the Peninsular War sapped Napoleon's strength. We tend to favour knocking out the props before assaulting the main building. The opposing school of thought believes in attacking the enemy where he is strongest. Here, then, was a revival of the old controversy between Westerners and Easterners of the First World War.

I have always believed that Mr. Churchill was right in his strategic appreciation which found expression in the Dardanelles campaign, and I still think that the slogging tactics of Haig on the Western Front were wrong. But quite apart from military considerations there were sound political reasons for pressing the attack on Italy. Italy was the pathway to Central Europe. We supported Russia wholeheartedly in her resistance to Hitler, but we were under no illusions as to possible developments after the War. Russia might be content with a settlement that rid her of the fear of an attack from the West – always an obsession with the Soviet leaders – or she might pursue a policy in Eastern Europe which would be in tune with the ideological imperialism of the Communists and the age-long ambitions of Russia. It would make a great deal of difference to Europe if the Western Slavs owed their deliverance to the democratic Powers and not to the totalitarians. One reason for the Americans opposing the exploitation of the victories in Italy was a failure to understand the importance of political strategy. They insisted on withdrawing resources from General Alexander in order to mount the invasion of Southern France. This was designed as a subsidiary operation to help the main attack on Germany, but it was an area of minor strategic importance, for success in the North would have sufficed to force a withdrawal in the South. The failure to press on with the attack from Italy left the deliverance of Central and South-Eastern Europe to the Russians. The same mistake was made later when American forces were halted and Czechoslovakia was not freed by the forces of democracy.

The other question which this book poses is whether General Eisenhower or General Montgomery was right in the plans for the exploitation of the victory in Normandy. Mr. Wilmot brings out very well the influences at work. Most important was the general American conception of strategy, which involved the deploying of the strongest possible forces on the whole front in order to smash the enemy all along the line. He shows how this is a natural result of the American habit of mind. The alternative is to bring to bear the greatest possible strength at one point and to smash the enemy there, with the result that his forces on the rest of the front are forced to give way. The German attack through the Ardennes in 1940 is a classical example of the second method; so also, on a smaller scale, is the Battle of El Alamein.

But wars are not fought on principles of cold logic. The actors are human beings, and national and personal factors come into play. Montgomery's plan would have meant that the decisive blow would have been delivered by forces under a British general, while the Americans would have supplied the greater number of troops. To have given General Patton a secondary rôle would have been difficult. The American Administration would have been criticized at home and, with an Election in the offing, this could not be disregarded. There was also the element of personal relationships. Montgomery had not the same sure touch in dealing with people of various nationalities as had Alexander and Eisenhower. He did not always realize the effect of his somewhat brusque methods. He became unpopular with the American Generals. It was unfortunate that this friction made some American Generals unwilling to serve under Montgomery, although he himself had offered to serve under Bradley, if his plan were accepted.

Mr. Wilmot shows how even General Eisenhower's plans were upset by the determination of General Patton to push on with his advance despite the directions given him. It is interesting to see, as the author points out, how the American custom of giving a very free hand even to subordinate commanders contrasted with the British practice. The Americans found it difficult to understand the control kept over major strategy by the Chiefs of Staff and the

British Cabinet. Mr. Wilmot states very fairly the arguments for both of these plans, but makes out a good case for believing that if Montgomery's plan had been adopted the War might well have been shortened and the political position in Europe during the post-war period much improved. It is perhaps inevitable that, as a member of the war-time Government, I should agree with his view.

Mr. Wilmot also shows how much Stalin gained at Yalta by the mistaken estimate of Russian reactions formed by President Roosevelt. The President seems to have thought that Britain was, and that Russia was not, an imperialist Power. He failed to understand that the word 'gratitude' does not find a place in the Communist vocabulary. In the East and the West he made unnecessary concessions to the Russians for which we are all paying to-day. In the event these concessions were given for nothing, for Russian help was not needed to defeat Japan, and in fact the Russians have profited in the Far East from victories won by the forces of democracy. They have reaped where they did not sow.

In this book full tribute is paid to the splendid services to the cause of freedom by our American Allies. I do not think that they will resent a frank discussion of points of political and military strategy on which the Allies, so united in purpose, took different views.

4

The Pleasure of Books

A room without books is a very dull affair, suggesting a hotel sitting room. When we found alternative accommodation in anticipation of receiving notice to quit 10 Downing Street, my wife made suitable provision for books. One end of our new drawing room was built up with shelves, while space was also found for two bookcases. My little study also was made ready to be lined with books.

There they stand, two or three thousand of them; the accumulation of many years – old friends and newcomers. Many of them are seldom or never opened, but I should hate to be without them. They are part of my life. The seniors have for the most part been bought, many of the juniors are gifts from the authors, while others are the fruits of inheritance.

They make a pleasant pattern of colour. Some are still fresh in bright bindings. I hate 'dust covers.' If they have come to stay why should they wear their overcoats? Others are much worn, even decrepit. The leather is mouldering and the backs have had to be repaired.

In moments of leisure I like to wander round and to pull out a book here and there, perhaps only for old times' sake; but there are some that I read again and again.

Looking through them one can see the influences of a lifetime. There are the oldest in the collection, two Rossettis and a Browning bought with ten shillings someone gave me when I was at school. They illustrate one ruling passion, for from the time that I could read, and even before, I have had an intense pleasure in poetry. Tennyson was an early love and is present in several volumes. How well I recall the shock of his death in 1892, for to a nine-year-old he appeared as immortal as W. G. Grace or Queen Victoria. The earliest Browning is a slim volume of *Men and Women*, the gift of a master at Haileybury. It soon had many companions. To that master, also, I am indebted for a fairly good knowledge of Shakespeare, thanks to the Reading Society which he entertained once a week. When I went to Oxford, which brought more money to spare and Blackwell's book-shop, more poets arrived. Swinburne and Morris join Rossetti as I am caught up in the Romantic Movement and fall in love with the Pre-Raphaelites.

Then appears the *Oxford Book of English Verse* in the India paper edition – a well-known veteran this, a beloved companion in two World Wars. I am indebted to Quiller Couch also for his delightful Cambridge lectures.

French and Italian poets are found there also, bearing witness especially to my interest in the Renaissance and the Risorgimento. Most of the classic English poets are there. Meredith was a comparatively late-comer. Masefield is there in full force and some of the Georgian poets, but here a halt is called. The moderns are absent. Is this a reflection on them or on me? I have tried but failed to appreciate them. Is it just advancing years that prevent me remembering a line of what they write? My mind is stored with poetry. On long journeys or during long nights in the trenches I have often set myself the task of repeating so many hundred lines of so many poets. Why can't I remember the moderns? Chaucer has only just arrived in readable form in Coghill's edition – a great pleasure. As I grow older I turn more and more to the greatest – to Milton and Shakespeare.

The Latin and Greek poets which I studied so assiduously at school only remain as a faint flavour. Horace alone holds his place in memory. For the rest I must depend on translations or on echoes of Greece and Rome that sound through the pages of our own English poets. It has always been a pleasure to me that places and times bring poetry to my mind. I remember Gallipoli recalling

> *Where the sea ridge of Helle hangs*
> *   heavier*
> *And east upon west waters break.*

and in Lemnos

> *And Limna's mountain rattles afar*
> *From the clatter of galloping feet.*

There is reciprocity here – place evokes poetry and poetry place. So, too, after enduring the Blitz, when our own planes went to Berlin, I thought of *Samson Agonistes* –

> *With winged expedition*
> *Swift as the lightning glance he executes*
> *His errands on the wicked.*

Those lines applied so well to the Nazis. I recall reciting this passage when dining with some exiled Danes during the War. A young man gave me his Milton as a memento. A few months later he fell in battle.

But enough of the poets. The novelists supply a fairly large contingent. *Tom Jones* is there and *Evelina*, but Scott is unrepresented. I never read more than half a dozen of his books, for he bored my generation. Thackeray too is absent. I read him in great gulps at school, but very little since. Dickens is there in vile mid-Victorian print, but he is there rather by inheritance than selection. I don't read much of him to-day, except *Pickwick*. Trollope is present in force, a recent acquisition fully read during an illness. The Brontës make a fine show in a presentation edition. Stevenson has most of a shelf to himself, as has Meredith, who shows signs of frequent use, though Hardy, once his equal in my affection, is seldom read now. But of all the classics, Jane Austen reigns supreme, read and re-read constantly, and near her sits *Cranford*, another very old favourite.

The shelves show an enthusiasm for Kipling, reflecting the imperialism of the turn of the century, but he has obviously been ousted from pride of place by Wells, Galsworthy, Arnold Bennett and Belloc, who rode so high in the Edwardian period. They indicate a complete change of outlook. Shaw, of course, is present, but with the dramatists. Chesterton is unrepresented, though his Falstaffian ghost may be somewhere in the background. It is always a nice point whether the works of a poet-novelist should be kept together or should file off with their respective peers. Belloc's poems in a little paper volume are with his novels. Here, too, for some odd reason is *The Hound of Heaven*, also in paper. Can it be that a common faith has drawn them together? Near these novelists are a rather mixed group of writers whom we used to regard as the novelists of exposure; Upton Sinclair, the American Winston Churchill, and others. The literary interest is seen here merging with the Socialist impulse.

We see this, too, in the high place assigned to William Morris, a prime favourite with a Socialist like myself, but also, in my view – especially in the *Defence of Guinevere* – a great poet. Hard by are sundry volumes of Ruskin, for it was through this gate that I entered the Socialist fold.

The next subject that holds a large place in my collection is history. From early days this has been a favourite study. Here will be found text books from the days when I took the Oxford History School, though I must admit that the less digestible matter, such as Stubb's *Charter*, was passed without regret to a younger brother. This is no orderly array. There is an odd volume of Gibbon now replaced by a handsome set recently inherited. I never read Gibbon right through until I was Prime Minister and found a fine edition at Chequers. I do not much care for the modern historians who spend a year or two on some obscure Pipe Roll. They are but 'honest hodmen' of history. The moderns are well represented, however, with Trevelyan, Bryant, Rouse, Seton Watson and Toynbee.

I love to stray into the byways of history and to read of curious episodes, such as the Latin Kingdom of Jerusalem. I have many subjects to which I always promise myself to devote more time when I have leisure, such as Roman Britain and the Anglo-Saxon Conquests – subjects where fascinating questions remain unanswered. When I was at Oxford I fell in love with my special period, the Renaissance, and that influence is clearly shown. Here is Addington Symonds *in extenso*, a prize bestowed by a generous College for getting a Second Class. There are sundry Italians, such as Machiavelli and Cellini and, of course, Dante.

Biographies now figure largely in this section, with an ever-growing contribution of the lives of men whom I have known. I retain much of what I read in the past, but I read it again illuminated by practical experience of Government which tends to make me more tolerant of those who bore the burden of responsibility in the past.

Economic and industrial history are, for the most part, dressed in more sober attire than *belles lettres* and tend to be relegated to the study where they join forces with Socialist, social reform and political works. Some of these might be called mere tools of the trade.

There is a massive series of the works of Sidney and Beatrice Webb, much studied in earlier days. There, too, are the Hammonds and the incomparable Tawney. Along with them are contributions to the social question, light and heavy. It is a nice point whether Douglas Cole's detective novels should be grouped with his serious work or relegated to the category of books which may be borrowed by the children without special leave. Here, too, are large collections of pamphlets, ammunition which I used to fire off at the street corner. There is a great deal of stuff on local government, much of it rather out of date to-day.

There is a big collection of maps and atlases. I like to pore over maps and to make in imagination the golden journey to Samarkand.

To come back to the drawing room. There are the serried ranks of the war books. World War I includes a fine collection of books on the Gallipoli campaign inherited from a brother who was, like myself, a participant in that tragic adventure. I revert to these quite often, weighing up the factors that made 'the little less and so far away' and thinking of the lads with whom I trained in 1914, so many of whom lie there in the Peninsula. Then there is the Second World War, where the ranks are led by the present Prime Minister's great series, with Eisenhower and Montgomery in close support. I have always been a keen student of military history. I recall that, in barracks in 1914, I read all Fortescue's history and Oman's *Peninsular War*. Close by are the peace books, almost as tragic as the war memoirs in their recollections of the vain hopes of the inter-war period. Next to these come books relating to foreign countries, quite a large collection of Americans of one kind and another, and a good deal of works on the Commonwealth. Back in the study is a whole series of volumes on India with the evidence given and the reports of the Simon Commission – all past history now.

There is much miscellaneous literature. Lord David Cecil, the best modern prose writer, and my old tutor, Ernest Barker, are favourites. And there is plenty of light reading, ranging from works of literary merit, which are honoured with a book-plate, and more fugitive books that have filled an idle hour. There are, too, the Penguins, Pelicans and the like, and the leading detective novelists, Agatha Christie, Wills Croft and Dorothy Sayers leading a regiment, the members of which are often detached for duty elsewhere.

Well, altogether it is a somewhat heterogeneous collection, indicating a catholic but by no means a comprehensive taste. Science is hardly represented and there is little theology, except the Bible, or philosophy. I have not sought out rare books or first editions though there are a few first and some fine limited editions, and three Morris *Kelmscotts*, the gift of some kind friends in the Socialist movement, who knew where my love abided. There are plenty of reference books from the *Encyclopædia Britannica* to *Wisden* and the *Rugby Football Annual*. Conference Reports are there in strength and are useful for reference. *Hansard*, so proudly displayed thirty years ago, has so increased in number that he has to be packed away discreetly behind the front ranks in the shelves.

I still have the old bookcase bought when I lived in Limehouse. It then housed my choicest volumes, but has now come down in the world, though it still holds some of the books that then held pride of place for they, too, have fallen from their high estate.

What a trouble it was when, divorced from their accustomed shelves, all the books were unloaded at short notice in our new abode! Hurriedly, they were put in the shelves, and for a time it was impossible to lay one's hand on a book when one wanted it. Only rough sorting could be done. Some obvious misalliances were immediately corrected. For instance, the *Life of Jesus* was removed from propinquity to Trotsky on Stalin in the biographical section. Much care has to be taken after spring cleaning to prevent such unfortunate meetings, but even now they are not really sorted out as I should wish.

There is the eternal conflict between size and content. There is the book that is just too large to fall in with its comrades of the same subject without a wasteful raising of the height of the shelf. There is the question whether books wearing the same uniform should fall in together in one bright regiment or be scattered. Should all the fine bindings be grouped together or should they appear here and there to leaven the lump? There is the problem of the very large book with fine illustrations, the gift of a distinguished foreigner. It won't fit into any shelf. Some day when I have time, I tell myself, there will be a great rearrangement, but already affinities have been formed which I shall not like to break.

Meanwhile, there they stand, a pleasure to look upon and behind them are ranked the shadowy forms of books read but not owned. Behind the orderly row of Stevensons and Buchans are Stanley Weymans and Anthony Hopes of boyhood. Stay! there is in being a Henty, but that was a Prep. School prize. There must be thousands of these ghosts from every one of which no doubt I have taken to myself something. There are, too, the ghosts of books which have been lent, but never returned. I still mourn a beautiful Browning, a twenty-firster handsomely bound and inscribed. Someone has got it. I look anxiously sometimes to see that no borrowed book has gained squatter rights. Only the other day I came across a second copy of *Kim*. Its first page was virgin, but on the second I found an inscription showing that it had been given to Jack on his birthday more than forty years ago. It had belonged to a Haileybury boy who, visiting our club in Stepney, had left it behind. Thereafter it had accompanied me to successive habitations. I returned it to its rightful owner, Marshal of the Royal Air Force Sir John Slessor. On the other hand, a kind neighbour who is interested in the works of de Guérin bought a copy in a second-hand book shop, discovered therein my father's book-plate and gave the book to me.

Well, a library is a joy not only because of the contents of the books or the brave show they make as decoration for a room, but because of their provenance, which revives many memories of the past.

5

Good Patriot and Bad Politician

I can recall very vividly the tragic days of 1940 when France dropped out of the fight for freedom. I recall the painful impression derived from the defeatist attitude of Petain and Weygand and the general attitude of despair. It was then that there emerged the man who embodied the old fighting spirit of France, General Charles de Gaulle. It is well, therefore, that we should have the opportunity of reading the General's own account* of the years 1940–42 during which, under his inspiring leadership, Free France took shape.

In the years which have since elapsed the figure of the General has to some extent become less vivid. He has become one of a number of French political leaders, and it is, perhaps, difficult to realize now how much France owes to this man.

In these memoirs the General not only gives an account of events, of the getting together of those Frenchmen who did not despair, but also draws a very clear picture of himself.

There emerges first of all the extremely able soldier, whose appreciation of the conditions of another major war were correct, but who failed to impress the old guard of generals who looked back to the last war and were obsessed with the doctrine of passive defence. It is clear that if the doctrines of de Gaulle had found favour with the politicians in power and with the French generals, there would have been an armoured mass of manœuvre able to deal with the German Panzer columns, and that France

*The Call To Honour by General Charles de Gaulle. Translated by Jonathan Griffin. Collins, 1955.

23

would have been spared the humiliation of the Armistice and the Vichy regime.

But we see, too, not merely the military technician but the dreamer, the romantic patriot, the man who had always the vision of France as something great, mystical and holy. He himself says, 'The emotional side of me tends to imagine France like the princess in the fairy stories or the Madonna in the frescoes as dedicated to an exalted and exceptional destiny. ... But the positive side of my mind also assures me that France is not really herself unless she is in the front rank. ... France cannot be herself without greatness.' The realization that Charles de Gaulle regarded himself as the expression of this romantic conception is the key to his character and accounts for the strength and weakness of the man.

In face of a France which had failed so lamentably, not merely through physical defeat on the battlefield, but also by lack of morale as contrasted with a Britain whose head was bloody but unbowed, he felt it his duty to assert in every possible way the greatness of France. With very slender forces and dependent on Britain for everything, he determined to claim for his movement as being the real France a position of equality with the Great Powers.

It is right to realize that it was essential for him to create his own 'mystique' in face of enormous difficulties. It is hard for us to realize the high prestige of Marshal Petain and the belief of many patriotic Frenchmen that somehow or other he would restore France to her old position. He was also, in the eyes of many, invested with legitimate power. French officials, I understand, clung to their allegiance to properly constituted authority as the one stable element. This was not unnatural in a country which had in the course of a century been an empire, a monarchy and a republic. To detach these men from Vichy was no easy task. de Gaulle, without denouncing the adherents of Vichy as traitors, had to create the idea that he and his associates were the real France.

Inevitably, his attitude was a source of extreme annoyance to his British and American Allies. He demanded to be treated as an equal ally and to be consulted fully and to be given early information of operations. There was not unnaturally some hesitation in giving full confidence to the rather scanty body of adherents who rallied to de Gaulle. This feeling was increased after the fiasco of Dakar, the failure of which was attributed in part to the loose talk of some of the French which was thought to have given the show away.

No doubt, also, there was lack of tact on the side of the Allies. It has never been easy for French and British to understand each other.

de Gaulle objected to any attempt to reach some *modus vivendi* with the Vichy Government yet, somewhat inconsistently, he was very sensitive where any collision with Vichy armed forces was concerned. They were after all Frenchmen though, for the time being, misguided. The British naturally regarded them with less tenderness.

But there was another cause of friction. The General was obsessed with the idea that we were imbued with a sinister imperialism and were seeking to take over the French Empire. He constantly inveighed against the intrigues of British agents.

A good example of this is seen in an incident which occurred before the Anglo-French attack on Vichy-held Syria. de Gaulle very wisely wished to prelude this attack with a declaration of the intention of France to bring to an end the Syrian mandate and to give independence to the Levant States.

When the British Government desired that the proclamation should be made jointly in the names of Great Britain and France, he reacted violently. He thought that it was an attempt to undermine French influence in the Levant in the interests of Britain. He clearly could not realize that the prestige of France was at a low ebb and that, if the declaration was to be effective with the populations of these States, it needed to be backed by the effective partner in the venture. He did not understand that imperialism was out of date and that Britain had no desire to be burdened with more dependencies, whether in Asia or Africa. It is interesting to recall that President Roosevelt was under the same delusion on the subject of British imperialism.

In the chapter called 'The Fall' we have the tragic events of 1940 seen from the standpoint of a fighting Frenchman which it is of interest to read with the story given in Sir Winston Churchill's *Their Finest Hour* and Sir Louis Spears's *Assignment with Catastrophe*. The General was, of course, all for continuing the fight, whether in Brittany or in North Africa. But no persuasion was effective and de Gaulle was left, as he says, to start from scratch in building up a resistance. He turned to the French Colonial Empire, and not without success. It is clear that in every instance much depended on the chance of finding in control the right man. The volume of documents which accompanies the memoirs shows the varying nature of the response. I remember at the time being struck by the fine spirit displayed by the African Governor, Felix Eboué, the Governor of Chad.

The General does not lack humour in his description of the working of what he calls the British machine when every influence was brought to bear upon him to adopt the British view. He certainly showed remarkable strength of mind in resisting pressure. He also, fairly enough, admits the great strain resting on the British when they stood alone.

I met General de Gaulle on a number of occasions during the War and was impressed by his personality but came to the conclusion that, despite all his other qualities, he lacked both political knowledge and insight. With his mind attuned to the past glories of France, he did not really appreciate the new forces moving in the modern world. This accounts, I think, for his failure to take advantage of the great position which he had won in the War to lead France in the post-War period.

The present volume only brings the story down to 1942 and concludes with the epic fight of the Free French at Bir Hakim. It had been hard for the General to get his troops employed in the North African campaign and one can easily sympathize with him in his intense satisfaction at this glorious feat of arms. General Koenig and his men had shown that Fighting France was a force to be reckoned with.

Until the day when he entered a liberated Paris and passed through the cheering crowds, this must have been de Gaulle's finest hour. No wonder that the book ends on a note of high emotion.

I shall look forward to further volumes with great interest. I am not in a position to judge the merit of the translation as I have not seen the French text, but the book is eminently readable.

6

Keir Hardie

The Labour Party is this year celebrating the hundredth anniversary of the birth of Keir Hardie, who is rightly regarded as its founder and whose name is remembered with affection and veneration. I recall seeing him for the first time at Temple Station on his way from Neville's Inn, where he lodged, to the House of Commons. I remember his sturdy figure dressed in tweeds, with a flowing red tie passed through a ring. With his beard already grey, he looked a venerable figure. Indeed, though he was then only fifty and was to die before he was sixty, we somehow always regarded him as an old man. It was not till later that I actually made his acquaintance at a Party Conference where I was a young delegate.

'Aristocrat'

It is worth while considering why the memory of Hardie is so dear to the Labour and Socialist Movement.

There is first his strong personality, which stamped itself on the Movement. There is his rugged independence, his honesty and his idealism. Bernard Shaw described him as the finest natural aristocrat. He expressed in himself the almost religious fervour which inspired the members of the Independent Labour Party. Then there is the fact that he was the first Labour Member of Parliament to be returned and to remain as an independent Member free from any connection with the old parties, for John Burns and Havelock Wilson soon sought refuge in the Liberal fold.

The 'Member for the unemployed,' as Keir Hardie was called, stood alone and braved unpopularity, not being afraid of incurring violent hostility, as when he asked the House of Commons to show as much sympathy with bereaved miners' wives as with a royal personage. Twice, in 1892 and in 1900, he was the only independent Labour Member returned, a forerunner indeed.

Strange Idea

In his struggle for the formation of an independent Parliamentary Labour Party he met formidable difficulties. First, the very idea of another party was strange in a Britain accustomed to the two-party system at a time when it could be said that

> ... *every boy and every gal,*
>   *That's born into this world alive,*
> *Is either a little Liberal,*
>   *Or else a little Conservative.*

He was accused of splitting the progressive vote. There was in the House of Commons a respectable body of trade unionists who belonged to the Liberal Party; even in 1906 they were nearly as numerous as the Labour Party members, and up till 1910 the majority of miners' Members, including leading personalities such as Thomas Burt and William Abraham, were Liberals. On the other hand there were the members of the Social Democratic Federation, with their narrow Marxian creed, to whom the I.L.P. and all its works were anathema because it refused to accept their shibboleths.

It was the great merit of Keir Hardie to recognise that merely to return working-class representatives to the House of Commons was not enough, for unless they were independent they would – as had already happened – become merely appendages of a predominantly capitalist party, but that, provided such a group were independent, it could not fail in time to become a Socialist Party. On the other hand, Keir Hardie saw that a professedly revolutionary party, couching its propaganda in Marxian terms and scornful of any alliance with the trade unions unless these also professed the Marxian creed, had little chance of success in Britain. He sought successfully to build up a party which should unite the class basis of the trade unionists with Socialist idealism.

History has justified his faith, for the Labour Representation Committee, with the modest aim of returning working-class candidates to Parliament, became the Labour Party: in a few years the Labour Party became Socialist, and in due course, without losing its fundamental basis, it became a national party, with representatives drawn from every stratum of society.

Many Strands

This firm belief in independence was not shared by all Labour Party leaders. I do not think that Ramsay MacDonald really had much faith in the party establishing itself as one of the two great parties in the State until 1924. He leaned towards coalition. There were, of course, many strands woven together to make the Labour Party – the Fabians, the Christian Socialists, the trade unionists, and some of the Social Democrats – but it was, I think, Keir Hardie and the I.L.P., of which he was the leader, that gave the party the distinctive character which differentiates it so definitely from most of the other Socialist Parties, except those of the Commonwealth and Scandinavia.

It was characteristic of Hardie that, while recognising the fact of the class struggle, he rejected the doctrine of the class war, and in company with Jean Jaurès spoke against it in the Second International. Though an impatient idealist, he worked for ameliorative reforms, rejecting the theory that increasing misery would bring about the social revolution he desired.

Nevertheless, despite his practical attitude, Hardie was much more a prophet than a Parliamentarian. His tenure of the chairmanship of the Parliamentary Party was short-lived. I think he recognised that Parliamentary leadership was not his *métier*.

Pacifist Views

He was a man of his time and had grown to middle age in the Victorian era. He held strong pacifist views. The failure of organised Labour to unite to stop the First World War was a great disappointment to him, and grief at the mass slaughter going on in the world hastened his end. It is useless to speculate as to what would have been his attitude towards modern developments, or how he would have reacted in the face of the rise of dictatorship.

One can say that he served well his generation, and one should not seek to use his name to approve or condemn the actions of those facing the problems of a different era. In my view, his fame rests on his having been the man who brought into being a Socialist Party consonant with the British way of life and very largely gave it its particular characteristics.

7

England My England

In the first volume of his history Sir Winston Churchill brought us in one broad sweep from the earliest times to the end of the Wars of the Roses, the close of the Middle Ages and the accession of the Tudor Dynasty. The pace has now slackened. The story of two centuries fills the 300 pages of this volume. One might, therefore, have hoped for a more comprehensive and balanced survey of the life of the British people, but one is disappointed. Ten pages suffice for a survey of world events including the Renaissance, the Reformation, the Counter-Reformation, and the discovery of the New World, just about as much space as is devoted to King Henry the Eighth's matrimonial adventures.

Politics and War, with religion in so far as it affects these paramount interests, are the absorbing topics. Other activities of the people receive slight consideration.

I had supposed that English literature was one of the glories of the English-speaking peoples and that that of the Elizabethan Age was one of the links that bind us to the peoples of North America, but there is little reference to it here. The Authorised Version of the Bible is duly noticed and Spenser's *Faerie Queene* is introduced apropos of Queen Elizabeth.

* * *

Shakespeare is fortunate, for, in connection with the conspiracy of Essex, he is mentioned as the author of a topical play, 'Richard II,' which was, we are told, to symbolise the dethronement of the Queen. Bacon, too, comes in as one of Essex's supporters. In the next century Milton does not even get a mention and shares in the neglect of the Cavalier poets and the Restoration dramatists.

31

One would have thought that the many-sidedness of the Elizabethans would have appealed to our protean author, but Raleigh is only the courtier and adventurer, not the poet or the author of a World History. Sidney is not even recalled in the story of the glass of water at Zutphen.

The philosophers fare no better. Bacon's *Novum Organum* and Hobbes's *Leviathan* are passed over in silence. Clarendon, however, as a Royalist historian and Dryden as a political satirist find a place. Equally neglected are the scientists. The founding of the Royal Society would, one might have thought, have interested its distinguished Honorary Fellow, or it might have been introduced in some account of the man who did more than anyone to build up the Royal Navy; but Samuel Pepys remains in the shadows and Charles the Second gets the laurels.

There were great advances in architecture during this period. The castle gave way to the Elizabethan house. Inigo Jones and Wren led the return to the classic style. English painters such as Kneller gave us pictures of the men and women of the time, but Sir Winston is as silent on the arts as on literature. Nor do we find any description of the changes of the mode of life of the people, yet this age sees the transition from the medieval to the modern way of life.

To turn to what is given us. In dealing with the Reformation and the Great Rebellion, Sir Winston shows himself much more in the character of an historian. Himself not much moved by doctrinal points, he seeks to deal fairly with Papists and Protestants, Anglicans and Non-conformists, though by nature he is averse from Puritanism.

Similarly, in the constitutional struggle, as a good parliamentarian he understands the cause for which Pym and Hampden fought, but he is also a sentimental Royalist and shares the emotions of the men who stood by Charles the First. He has a good hearty dislike for dictators. Cromwell he can admire as a man of action and a soldier, but the sack of Drogheda puts him beyond the pale. He considers him in lasting discord with the genius of the English race, but here again he shows a fine objectivity:–

Without Cromwell [he writes] there might have been no advance, without him no collapse, without him no recovery.

*Amid the ruins of every institution, social and political, which
had hitherto guided the island race, he towered up gigantic,
glowing, indispensable, the sole agency by which time could be
gained for healing and regrowth.*

I should have expected from so great an authority on military
matters rather more appreciation of Cromwell's military genius.
He was not merely a great tactician and strategist, but the greatest
trainer of troops, whose like was not to be found until Sir John
Moore, while his Articles of War remained till recently the basis
of military discipline.

* * *

I think if Sir Winston had lived in the seventeenth century he
would have been one of the foremost parliamentarians. He would
have shed no tears for Strafford, but when war broke out he
would have stood for the King and charged with Prince Rupert,
while in his old age he would have joined in the invitation to
Dutch William.

There is a chapter on the beginnings of the American colonies
which might well have been expanded. Sir Winston says that owing
to the Civil War the colonies were left to grow for nearly a quarter
of a century. One would like to be told more about that period
when the foundations of a great nation were laid. Eighty thousand
English-speaking people crossed the Atlantic in a few decades.
Some analysis of this great company of adventurers would have
been interesting and also some account of how they fared.

When we come to the revolution of 1688, interest quickens for
the Churchill family which, already noticed in the person of the
first Sir Winston, now reappears in the persons of Arabella and
John, preluding the great events of the age of Anne which John
will dominate.

This is as it should be, for this history is mainly important for
the light which it throws on the author's reactions to the past. It
might indeed be better called 'Things in history which have
interested me.'

A History of the English Speaking Peoples.
Vol. 2: The New World by Winston S. Churchill. Cassell, 1956.

8

Blue Stocking in Action

A hundred years ago Beatrice Webb was born. She, with her husband Sidney, constituted one of the most remarkable partnerships in history. When John Burns was told that these two distinguished social investigators had become engaged to be married, he was asked, 'What do you think will be the result?' He replied: 'A great big blue book,' and he was right. Indeed it is as difficult to separate the contributions of these two to the social developments of the times in which they lived as to assess the contributions of a father and mother to the making of a distinguished family of sons and daughters.

Yet Beatrice Webb herself was a remarkable personality and even without her husband would have made a great impact on the age.

The eighth of the famous daughters of Richard Potter, the railway magnate, she was brought up in a circle of serious Victorians. A friend of Herbert Spencer, she mingled with many distinguished men and women. It seemed at one time that she might have become the third wife of Joseph Chamberlain. It was perhaps as a result of the ending of this attachment that she embarked on her life work. She helped Charles Booth in his great survey of London poverty. She had practical experience of life as a wage earner and she wrote a penetrating study of the cooperative movement in Britain before the famous partnership began.

Back-Room Socialism

Thenceforward there came from their joint efforts a whole series of books which profoundly influenced the current of public opinion generally and especially affected the outlook of the men and women of the Socialist and trade union movements.

The History of Trade Unionism and Industrial Democracy threw a new light on the subject for students of sociology and gave the trade unionists not only an historical background, but a theoretical basis for their own practical work. Another great series dealt with local government, again breaking new ground for the historian and student of politics. These studies also had great importance for the rising Socialist and Labour movement. The Socialist unable to make more than a small breach in the citadel of power at Westminster got elected to the local council and, thanks to the Webbs, was far better instructed in the problems of municipal administration and far more alive to its possibilities than his opponents of the old parties. By these works and many others, and by the Fabian tracts the young enthusiasts of the Socialist movement were armed for their fight against the existing order of things.

In the nineteenth century there was a far more meagre supply of data than is now afforded by Government publications.

No Utopian

The careful investigation of facts and their publication had great educational value. Further than this their publication and the concentration on a practical consideration of existing institutions and as to how they could be used to effect wide changes contributed very much to the particular character of the British Labour movement, turning it away from vague utopian dreams on the one hand and on the other from the arid doctrinal discussions which were a feature of some continental parties.

A decisive event in Beatrice Webb's life was her membership of the Royal Commission on the Poor Law in the years 1905–09. She was the dominant personality of that distinguished body and inspired the famous Minority Report which may be regarded as the seed from which later blossomed the welfare state.

Her decision to launch a crusade for the adoption of the principles of the report brought her much more into the public eye than before. Hitherto she had been content to work mainly through permeation and by endeavouring to influence the influential. Her impact on the rank and file of the Labour movement had not been great.

In her crusade she enlisted a large body of workers, particularly of the younger generation, and pursued it with tremendous vigour. She was a most persuasive talker and had the gift, invaluable in a propagandist, of implying that agreement with her contentions was evidence of high intelligence in her hearer.

Personal Impression

As one who enlisted under a banner, I recall her very well in the full vigour of middle life sitting on the arm of a sofa throwing out ideas which Sidney elaborated on paper in his large, clear handwriting. Her own was almost illegible.

I think that in their earlier days the Webbs put too much faith in their powers of persuading non-Socialists of prominence to support Socialist measures without fully realizing what they were doing.

I think that the failure of the Liberal Government to adopt the Minority Report and her experience that the most whole-hearted workers came from the Labour movement gradually convinced her that the changes she desired could not come from the Liberal Party and that it was to a Labour Party that she must turn.

This feeling was accentuated by the break up of the Liberal Party and the progress of the Labour Party, first to being the Opposition and then to forming a Government.

Throughout the disappointing period between the two wars when the Labour Party held office without power, Beatrice Webb worked hard to help the Parliamentary Party to get together, and particularly she tried to get the wives of members to meet. She was here trying to get for the Labour Party the kind of thing which the old parties had, but she was not very successful.

Most Labour members' wives lived in the country, and I do not think that she was really at ease with ordinary working people. She was too much the intellectual and did not understand the thought processes of people with a different background from her own.

Faulty Judgment

She underestimated or did not appreciate the extent to which a movement such as that of the British Labour Party is influenced by sentiment. I think her judgment of people was often faulty, for this reason.

It was, I think, this failure to understand the importance of the human factor in society as against the mechanics that led these two highly intelligent people to misunderstand so gravely the nature of the Russian Communist régime. Mrs. Webb certainly never realized what a deadly thing was the role of 'The Party' in the Communist régime.

I remember on several occasions she pressed on me the need for a dedicated cadre of workers on the Jesuit model which would be the mainspring of the new order in society. It indicated, I thought, a lack of confidence in what ordinary men and women could do in a democracy.

These illusions were perhaps due to the coming on of old age and should not be allowed to detract from the work which she did in her prime. She could have no more done the work that Hardie and Lansbury with their evangelistic fervour did than they could have done the Webbs' work of research.

The peaceful revolution in Britain was the outcome of the demands of the workers for a juster society and of the willingness of people from the privileged classes to admit the justice of the demands and to help them to realize them.

The social conscience which stirred in Victorian England inspired many men and women in diverse ways to serve others. Among them Beatrice Webb will always hold a high place.

9

A Good Man

Here in a sumptuous volume of eight hundred pages is the official life of King George VI* who reigned for fifteen difficult and troubled years, written by a distinguished historian who has had to cover both the public and private life of the monarch. I have heard it said that an Australian, reading the memoirs of the Duke of Windsor in a small country town, exclaimed: 'My God weren't we lucky!' Despite the many amiable qualities of the Duke most people would agree that Britain was extremely fortunate in having at the head of the country and the Commonwealth King George and his consort Queen Elizabeth.

I was privileged to serve him as a Minister of the Crown for eleven years and for more than six of them as Prime Minister. Having read many lives of previous occupants of that position, and having studied how they fared under monarchs as different as George IV and Queen Victoria, I have often thought how lucky I was to serve one who was the model of what a constitutional King should be. I recalled at Oxford reading the works of Bagehot and other eminent Victorians on the British Constitution and learning that the King reigns but does not rule. It was not till long afterwards that I realized that Queen Victoria was far from accepting the role which they described. The reality had to wait for George V and his son. I learn from this book that George VI read Bagehot at Cambridge and must certainly have marked and inwardly digested his doctrine. Hereditary monarchy has disappeared from the greater part of the Continent of Europe

King George the Sixth, His Life and Reign by J. W. Wheeler-Bennett, Macmillan, 1958.

except in Scandinavia and The Low Countries. The reason why it has maintained its position in Britain and large parts of the Commonwealth is largely on account of the characters of the monarchs who have reigned from 1837, and especially of the last two Georges.

The position of a monarch in a modern democratic State does not call for the possession of exceptional ability; indeed to have it might be rather a disadvantage. What is needed is someone of good intelligence, character and judgment, and a high sense of duty. All these qualities, as is well brought out in this book, King George possessed in a marked degree.

Ordinary people are interested in the Royal Family and its doings not because they are people of a different fibre but because they are people like themselves or what they would like to be. This was once well expressed to me by a small boy in the East End of London who said: 'Some people think as how the King and Queen are different from us, but they are really just the same, only they can have a relish with their tea'. Undoubtedly there is a very real devotion to the Crown not only in Britain but in the old Dominions overseas, while perhaps the enthusiasm is strongest in the great American Republic. People like a bit of pomp and circumstance which takes them out of dull everyday life to the fairy stories of their childhood.

Fifty years ago most people of Left-wing views were theoretically in favour of a republic. Outside a handful of Communists and a few 'intellectuals' there are very few today. There are too many examples in the world of the ease with which a President or a general can make himself a dictator in a republic to make anyone think that a republican form of government is a safeguard for freedom and democracy, while there are plenty of examples of great progress in the application of the principles of democracy and socialism under limited monarchies. Jimmy Maxton at the time of the Abdication did indeed move a republican motion, but he was not serious. I recall him telling me that he saw no advantage in substituting a bourgeois President for a King. Incidentally, I think that our author overrates the damage done to the Monarchy by the Abdication crisis.

In fact there are very real advantages in hereditary monarchy. It avoids the upset of a periodic election and the choosing of candidates, a process which in the United States does not seem very edifying. It gives the people someone to whom they can give loyalty, who is not a party politician and the choice of a section of the people. The King is a symbol of unity in a democracy where, quite rightly, there are contending parties. There is a story which illustrates this. A British general was entertaining an American general at dinner. He gave the toast of the King, adding piously: 'God bless him'. He then gave the toast of the American President, who was a Democrat, and the American general, a Republican, responded 'The President, God help us'. Further, in a Commonwealth of such diversity of peoples as our own, the choice of a President who would commend himself to all presents great difficulties. Admitting that hereditary right is illogical and, if you will, an out-of-date anomaly in a modern State, nevertheless its justification is that it works well in practice. The only valid objection is that it promotes snobbery, but this is a general human failing and I have yet to learn that it does not exist in republics. George VI had not expected to succeed to the Throne when he did and, quite apart from the pain of parting with a well-loved brother, was very far from wishing it. He would much have preferred the life of a sailor or of a country gentleman to which his natural tastes inclined him. He felt that he had not been trained for the job. It is interesting that Lord Mountbatten told him, as his father had told George V when the Duke of Clarence died, that there was no better preparation for the job than service in the Royal Navy. There was indeed much advantage in having followed a professional career which enabled him to mix with his fellows on far more equal terms than is possible for the heir to the Throne.

He went to Osborne and Dartford. The brooding presence of the old Queen still hung over George V, but as the Duke of Windsor pointed out he and his brothers were free from it. None the less it was strong enough to prevent them from going to school and made the future King's education an affair of tutors. This tradition has now been broken in respect of Prince Charles. George VI was by nature a shy man and the habit of his father in inflicting upon him frequent pi-jaws did not help. Indeed it looks as if George V, despite his great affection for his children, was not a very understanding father. Furthermore, this son had the serious disability of stammering. Many physicians failed to effect a cure and it was not until he was thirty that a Mr. Logue was able to suggest a method of overcoming it. It says much for his determination that he practised the method and overcame the trouble, though to the end of his life certain words were difficult and had to be avoided in drafting the Speech from the Throne, while the word 'Approved', which had to be said so often in the Privy Council, still needed an effort.

King George lived in times of rapid change and it is greatly to his credit that he adapted himself to new conditions and to the passing away of an order to which he was naturally attached. It must have been hard for him to accept the gradual departure of the old Britain in which he had been brought up, with its class distinctions, great country houses and the whole Victorian set-up, and to see a more democratic way of life coming in, together with the supplanting to a large extent of the old ruling class. Yet I never knew him to complain or repine. Equally readily he accepted the change over from an Empire to a Commonwealth. During my Ministry the Imperial Crown of India was relinquished. He raised no objection. One can imagine how Queen Victoria or even Edward VII would have greeted such a proposal.

The King had a very high sense of duty. In the First World War ill health prevented him from seeing much active service afloat, and he fretted because he was not sharing to the full what other young men of his age were experiencing. In the Second World War, he wanted to do more than he could. He stayed in London throughout the bombing raids and rather welcomed the fact that Buckingham Palace was hit as well as lesser dwellings. I think that he was prone to worry a great deal over what was happening to his people, for whom he felt such great responsibility. He was excellent company, with a quick mind and a very lively sense of humour. He was an admirable host and could put the most diffident at ease. His judgment was excellent and I cannot recall his putting a foot wrong. He often had happy ideas as in establishing his Annual Camp where boys of varying social backgrounds met together. His own idea of giving the George Cross to Malta and the special award to Stalingrad are other examples. One would gather from this book that as a boy he was rather disinclined to hard work, but he became extremely diligent. I always found him completely up-to-date in his knowledge of State papers and Foreign Office telegrams. I can recall many meetings with him, both formal and informal, for he had a happy gift of informality: yet I cannot recall any occasion on which a difference arose between us. Although he had a progressive mind I have no doubt that some of the measures of the Labour Government were distasteful to him, yet he never raised objections; nor do I ever recall his questioning an appointment. It is well brought out in this book how throughout his life he grew into his responsibilities and never failed to meet the challenge of a situation. He was indeed a most attractive character and a very good man.

It is difficult to write an official biography and to get just the right balance between public and private matters. Mr. Wheeler-Bennett had not only to write the story of a life but to set it in the perspective of the time in which his subject lived. This task is particularly difficult in a reign so crowded with events. I am inclined to think that rather more of the public background might have been given which will be increasingly important as the present passes into history. Much also depends on the point of view of the historian as to what he thinks important. For instance, the tragedy of the economic crisis of the early 'thirties, and the intense misery experienced by so many of the workers, is hardly mentioned. It was, he says, a period of great stability for the British Monarchy. One gets the impression that so long as there is a predominantly Conservative Government in office all is well. Similarly he deals extremely gently with the faults of the Governments preceding the Second World War and is apt to accord them a greater measure of popular support than they actually had. He states that Mr. Neville Chamberlain's policy from first to last received the whole-hearted support of a considerable majority of his fellow-countrymen. He offers no evidence for this remarkable statement. He is, I think, apt to take the views of the popular Press too seriously. His general approach is rather coloured by his personal views. He deals as fairly as he can with the Labour Government, but clearly regards the accession of Labour to power as a regrettable lapse from normality.

Mr. Wheeler-Bennett writes well and his narrative holds the attention. There are many good illustrations, the best of which is, I think, Mr. Gunn's conversation piece of the family at Royal Lodge. This is right, as the background of the King's life was his happy family relations. I like the remark of the American Senator to him: 'My you're a great Queenpicker'. There are useful appendices, particularly one dealing with the monarch's private secretary. Not one of these distinguished men did a better job than Sir Alan Lascelles.

I have detected only one error of fact. In the 1940 Government the three Service Ministers were not in the Cabinet, nor was the Chancellor of the Exchequer, Sir Kingsley Wood.

10

Montgomery: My Assessment

Field-Marshal Montgomery was a great soldier: great, in my opinion, not only by the standards of his generation, but in the eye of history. He is – as I am – an admirer of Oliver Cromwell. To my mind he is not unworthy of comparison with Cromwell. Both had three qualities not often found together: they were brilliant trainers of troops, superb battle-commanders, and were strategists of the highest order. Both were more than consummate military technologists: both of them not only were inspired and made dynamic by profound religious belief, but relied on expressing this, day in day out, for their moral authority over their men.

Though both men believed, as captains as well as puritans, in the strictest outward as well as inward discipline, and would tolerate no insubordination, both were in a curious way more democratic than many of the distinguished commanders around them. Cromwell preferred the 'plain russet-coated captain' to the man who owed his position to birth or wealth. Montgomery had no use for the old school tie or the old boy network, told his men to wear what they liked – though he once officially drew the line at top hats – and discouraged his men from respecting red tape, pomp and the trappings of authority.

Thinking Fast and Coolly

Like Cromwell, he could think fast and coolly in the heat of battle, and manipulate masses of men and armour with a tactical speed and confidence which must have seemed magical to the enemy. Like Cromwell, Montgomery frequently scored by doing something which the enemy thought impossible. He had that readiness, at the precisely right moment, guided by an intuition, to, as he puts it, 'throw his bonnet over the moon' and commit everything to the supreme effort.

Montgomery, too, personally exhorted his men before the battle and sent them battle-orders, to be read down to a man, sprinkled with quotations from the Psalms, and dedicated to the 'Lord mighty in battle.' His orders are a curious mixture of romanticism, tough Officer-Commanding talk, and prep. school slang – phrases like 'God bless us all' and 'We shall hit them for six' landing up in most stimulating juxtaposition. Anyway, he got himself across, as few generals have, to the very heart of the fighting man. Wolfe did it. Marlborough did it. Not many have.

Clumsy Handling of the Press

Cromwell did not give press conferences. Sometimes it would have been better if Montgomery had not, as he admits himself. He made a clumsy job of the big press conference he held on January 7, 1945. His object was to try to improve Anglo-American relations. Though it wasn't entirely his fault, he left Anglo-American relations considerably worse. On the whole, however, he got himself and his men a very good press, and this was good not only for them but for the morale of the men and women at home.

Another feature he has in common with the great commanders was that he never allowed himself to get bogged down in detail. He left the detail to his staff, having first given them the central plan himself. He could then, as he did, go to bed and sleep soundly every night, kicking up a row if anybody woke him unless it was absolutely necessary. His mind was always fresh and free for the emergency. He says at one point in his book* that some Cabinet Ministers and generals allow themselves to get bogged down in detail, and that this is bad. I quite agree. There is no excuse for it.

His contribution to the winning of the war was of the highest order. It was crucial. That he did what he did was important, but tremendously important was that he began to do it at a critical

*The Memoirs of Field Marshal Montgomery. Collins, 1958.

time. We badly needed a victory. He has been belittled as an exhibitionist, but what he did was done of set purpose. It was indeed a reversion to the days of small forces when a leader *led* his men into battle. A different idea was current in World War One. It was believed that a general should be aloof lest the sight of a battle should unnerve him, as, so it was said, was General Buller in the South African War. The result was, as I well remember as an infantry officer, we knew no general senior to our Divisional General. Corps commanders, army commanders, were quite unknown. The personality of Haig never in my experience got across to the troops. The general impression was that, whenever the mud and blood were flying, the generals would be well behind the lines.

Montgomery had exactly the opposite ideas about generals and men, and in 1942 these crashed into effect. He found Eighth Army with their tails down. He changed the whole atmosphere right away. He was encouraged to publicise himself, of course (though later he was discouraged a bit), but the idea that he should do so was his, and the credit must go to him. Perhaps a man who was not an exhibitionist could not have made such a great job of it. In that case, we should be grateful for that trait in his character.

Judged simply as a personality he is certainly one of the most interesting men I have ever met. I have always liked him very much. He is great fun, with a delightful sense of humour, of a rather boyish kind, as comes out abundantly in this excellent book of his. He always liked to have things his own way, of course, and sometimes this brought him into conflict with anybody under whom he had to work. I do not think this was a mean or even superficial trait in his character. I think it comes from deep inside him, and has to do with the tremendous conflict he and his mother lived in with regard to each other when he was a lad, a conflict which he describes with fairness and insight in his book, and which may have led to the fact, as he puts it himself, that apart from his wife, who died after ten years of marriage, 'women had never interested me.'

Behaved Almost Like a Child

However, and this is perhaps not always appreciated, after Montgomery had his row, or argument, with his superior, and had got the thing off his chest, he could work loyally under him to the end. I sometimes feel about him that, in fact, he was at his best as a No. 2 and was really, in the midst of these rows, trying to find that superior, stable figure in whom he could put his boyish and devoted trust – as he did with Alanbrooke, Alexander, and Eisenhower.

Some people have got it into their heads that, because he did not drink or smoke and went to bed every night, if he could, at ten, and generally was a pretty ascetic character, he was cold and chill. Nothing of the kind. Anybody who thinks so should read the pages in his Memoirs which describe his relationship with his wife. They are poignant. I always thought him quite an emotional person, usually in a quite naïve and almost boyish kind of way. Indeed, some of the difficulties he gave his colleagues and his superiors were due not so much to a profound intellectual disagreement with their views as, I think, to the fact that occasionally he could, and did, behave almost like a child.

He showed himself a much more tolerant man than is often supposed. It is not surprising that he thought the world of Winston – Winston thought the world of him. But it is not generally appreciated that he worked very well with, and expressed respect for, many people with whom he had far less in common. In this book he has said some very complimentary things, for instance, about members of the Labour Government, with whom from time to time he came into conflict. As Prime Minister, I myself had to give him more than one tick-off, and once I had to give him a really good raspberry. But he took it well, and takes it well looking back on it.

His Liking for Respect

Though he liked to choose his own subordinates and to have around him only men whom he knew respected him – a tendency which many great soldiers and civilians have displayed – this does not mean that his deputies and satellites were minor editions of himself. He chose as his Chief of Staff – and what a fine appointment it turned out to be – a man, de Guingaud, whom he describes in the book as fond of wine and gambling and good food, and who certainly did not care to go to bed at ten o'clock each night. 'We were complete opposites,' he says in the book. Bill Williams, his Chief of Intelligence, again a magnificent choice, was a little-known and quite unspectacular-seeming Oxford don.

One thing that always struck me about Montgomery was that he seemed remarkably free from prejudices in favour of or against people on the basis of class, social background, political or spiritual commitment. I suppose it was because he himself was so individualistic. And he says in his book that he was the cat that walked alone largely because of his feeling of isolation in his family on account of the tension between him and his remarkable mother.

Against Gifts for Generals

Whatever the underlying reason, he was remarkably good at 'making contact' with people of very different social backgrounds. There was a peculiar 'classlessness' about him which I am sure impressed the ordinary soldier. I like Montgomery for not taking a penny from his parents after he had left Sandhurst and for, when his financial circumstances were altogether different, coming to the same arrangement with his son. Like me, he strongly opposed the idea of giving generals gifts of money after the war. He is not a snob, and is more of an egalitarian than he often sounds.

At school, as he tells us in his book, his nickname was 'Monkey.' I can quite understand why they called him that. In his school magazine there is a piece about him which he reproduces. His school fellows are advised to be careful of their relations with the monkey, especially when playing football. 'It is vicious, of unflagging energy, and much feared by the neighbouring animals ... it is advisable that none hunt the monkey.' His sense of humour occasionally got him into trouble. As he frankly tells us, he got into serious trouble at Sandhurst because as a jape he set fire to the tail of a brother cadet's shirt. Being a teetotaller, of course, he did not even have the excuse of being drunk when he did it.

Challenged by Auchinleck

On the whole, it is a fair book, as books of this kind go. But certain impressions, of events and personalities, emerge which I think could stand correction. General Auchinleck, for instance, gets far less than his due. Montgomery does not make enough allowance for Auchinleck's difficulties being due to shortage of equipment, and to considerations of overall strategy, as they existed at the time. General Auchinleck has already publicly disputed certain statements that Montgomery has made to the effect that Auchinleck had turned his back on the possibilities of a battle like El Alamein, but was thinking in terms of standing still or retreating. Auchinleck cites official documentary proof.

Montgomery does not sufficiently note that whereas previous generals had been working on a shoestring, he took over when everything was being provided for a really big drive forward. The fact is that Montgomery got everything he asked for. He was given not only the guns, and the equipment, and the advice, but he was given the officers that he asked for (he was asked to retain only one general against his will).

In very many hundreds of words about El Alamein, and how he won it, Montgomery says exceedingly little about the complete change in the scale of his fighting power, effected by civilians and generals at home and abroad whom he does not mention. This section of the book, I think, could do with many more references to the role that Alexander played. He is referred to, all right, many times, and with great respect and affection: but always as some rather remote fellow in the background, whom Monty would get hold of when he wanted some moral support in dealing with the War Cabinet, or in order to ask for something further to be done. An uninformed reader might almost reach the conclusion that Alexander was a kind of glorified quartermaster – welfare officer, somewhere back in Cairo, instead of what he was: the great soldier-statesman under whose aegis, and within the framework of whose guidance and control, Montgomery was allowed to conceive and execute the battle plans which won the tactical and strategical victories which cleared the Germans out of North Africa.

I believe that Alexander, in the field, might not have done as well as Montgomery did: but I think that if Alexander had been the Supreme British Field Commander in Europe, he might have done as well as Montgomery did there without running into as much difficulty as Montgomery did in dealing with the Americans.

Again, in the case of Alanbrooke, as C.I.G.S., though Montgomery speaks of him with the greatest respect and affection, I do not think that readers of this book would properly understand that it was Alanbrooke who was responsible for the total situation in which Monty's brilliant achievements were but one – even if the most important – factor.

When the changes in command in North Africa were made, General Gott, who had a fine fighting record, was chosen to command Eighth Army. Gott was killed in an aeroplane accident and Montgomery was brought from England to take his place. It was, therefore, an accident of war which brought the right man to the right place. Good as Gott was, he was, as he said himself, a tired man. Montgomery was exactly the horse for the course.

A Good Turn for History

If some parts of the book obscure things as they really were, others admirably clarify them. Monty has done himself – and history – a good turn in making clear the exact nature of the bone of contention between himself and Eisenhower in 1944 immediately after the Battle of Normandy. What Montgomery wanted was a 'concentrated thrust' from the eastern or left flank of the Allied Forces in Northern France, aiming directly at the Ruhr and Berlin and securing the Northern French ports, and those of Holland, Belgium and North Western Germany on the way. Eisenhower favoured the broad front strategy with a two-pronged attack. The two conceptions are admirably illustrated in the book by maps.

Now, in the discussions which ultimately led to Montgomery's ideas being rejected, his notion of a 'concentrated thrust' was badly served by those who talked of it in terms such as 'pencil thrust' and 'narrow front.' Montgomery was very incensed at the time by this. If it had been a question of making a pencil thrust, as he says in the book, he would have opposed it himself. It was a big punch forward, not unlike those at Mareth and Alamein, that he had in mind. And to turn down his plan as though it had advocated a 'pencil thrust' was unjustifiable and must have been maddening for him.

Personally, I think that Montgomery's plan should have been adopted. If it had been, we should have knocked out the

Germans. This is, I believe, the view of some of the German generals. We should have got to Berlin altogether sooner than we did – well before the Russians – with immense effects on the post-war situation. The fact is that the British Government and Chiefs of Staff strongly favoured Montgomery's plan because they had a much better idea than the Americans of the real nature of Russian imperialism and of the importance of getting to Berlin before the Russians did. We had only very reluctantly agreed to the American plan for the invasion of France from the south – the operation 'Anvil.' It entailed the weakening of Alexander's forces designed for the conquest of Italy and possible progress to Vienna. It also influenced Eisenhower in his preference for the two-pronged attack. The Americans did not understand Eastern Europe or Stalin, who naturally warmly approved of Anvil. Montgomery's correct military strategy was in line with the political views of the War Cabinet.

Unfortunately, it was partly Montgomery's own fault that his advice was not taken. He frequently showed so little sympathy with the difficulties of getting the Americans to put in major efforts in Europe, and not switch them to the Far East, that in any argument in which Anglo-American military relations were involved, his views were at something of a discount.

The Commander in the Field

The best half of the book is the first half. In this Montgomery is describing himself as a commander in the field, doing a commander in the field's work. He writes simply, frankly, vividly, and in the egotistical vein in which, I suppose, a book about complex subjects has to be written if it is to get across to the general reader. I would not be surprised if this first half of the book, roughly speaking up to the victory in Normandy, became a classic of its kind. In this part of the book, of course, Montgomery is talking about things which he not only did brilliantly but which he perfectly comprehends. The second part of the book is not so good: here Montgomery has reached the soldier-statesman level. Hereafter, to my mind, the book makes less of an impact on the reader, not only because its author has to deal with what, clearly, are some failures, but because he has to deal with affairs which he did not properly grasp.

Montgomery was appointed C.I.G.S. in 1946. He was not really well fitted for the post, though, to be fair to him, it was not for lack of effort, or capacity, but because his individualism and non-conformity had taken him too far for him to be able to turn back and adapt himself to the different set of requirements which a successful Chief of the Imperial General Staff must satisfy. A good C.I.G.S. must be a good committeeman, able to reconcile conflicting points of view, co-operate with men whom he does not necessarily regard as superior, or even equal, and while securing the trust of his soldiers, be able to relate their wishes, advice, and needs to those of the body politic.

A Difficulty in Co-operating

Montgomery was honest and loyal, but he could not easily co-operate. His judgment, too, seemed less good than it had been – he told me, for instance, that if there was a flare-up in the Middle East, the Arabs would 'hit the Jews for six' into the sea. We soon saw who did the hitting. Though, unlike many of his generals, he had gone into World War Two determined not to fight it with the mental attitude and weapons of World War One, yet he seemed to contemplate a third world war in twenty years or so with masses of men fighting on the Continent. He was annoyed at the Labour Government not accepting his views, but later he recognised the vast technological changes which have altered the character of war.

Admirable as leader of a task force, he found it difficult to adapt himself to the role of one of the technical advisers to a civil Government. His strictures on the post-war set-up in the sphere of defence really show the defects of his good qualities.

I find him rather lacking in self-criticism and insight about this, though these are two qualities in which on the whole he is well endowed.

Alexander Saw the Danger

Alexander, incidentally, stood in great contrast to this after the war. He told me that he did not wish to have another military post because of the danger that he would always be thinking of the last war – not looking to the future.

I was rather disappointed with Montgomery in this respect. He showed lack of appreciation of the economic position of the country, which necessitated very careful balancing of effort in the civil and military spheres. Montgomery in the war had always got what he asked for. Field-Marshal Slim, who had to make do with leavings in his Burma campaign, was better fitted to understand the difference between the desirable and the possible. Being able to do this is, of course, the test of the soldier-statesman as opposed to the commander in the field. On this basis, I think Alanbrooke, Alexander and Slim superior to Montgomery as all-round soldiers.

As is clear from his recent speeches, he seems doomed to judge politicians and policies entirely in terms of whether they give him, or prevent him from having, the particular military facilities and opportunities which he happens to want at the time. If the Welfare State, for instance, means that Montgomery does not get exactly the type of armaments that he considers ideal, then he is against the Welfare State.

The fact is that though Montgomery, with a penetrating mind, thought through his military problems up to the level of army commander, he did not think them through on the higher levels. He knew the importance of good welfare arrangements for building up the morale of his Eighth Army, and nobody understood the need for establishing that morale better than he did. He doesn't seem to have as clear an idea of the importance of morale and welfare in the larger socio-political field. This is where, to my mind, he falls behind others of our generals.

Curious Ideas on Diplomacy

He has some curious ideas about generals and diplomacy, too. In 1947, he went off on a tour of various countries, as C.I.G.S. He admits himself in the book that he appeared to be an Ambassador Extraordinary. In fact, to me it seemed as though he was behaving like an Ambassador Plenipotentiary. For instance, he discussed an alliance between Britain and the Soviet Union in a private talk with Stalin. He meant no harm, of course. He just did not understand where to draw the line.

As a No. 2 in Nato, however, Monty was a great success. His readers will find he had thought a great deal about Western

Europe, and particularly about its politico-military role in the post-war world. He describes the influence upon his thinking of some advice given him by General Smuts on the eve of D-Day, to the effect that after the war Europe would disintegrate unless it was supplied with a structure on which to rebuild itself. France had failed dismally, said Smuts, according to Montgomery. 'Britain must stand forward as the cornerstone of the new structure ... Britain is a continental nation ... Britain must remain strong and keep small, but highly efficient, forces which are capable of rapid expansion.' Montgomery turned out to be remarkably 'continental minded,' and as a result, I am sure, has performed a considerable service to the free world.

Some books which have been written by generals about the last war have raised the question of the relations between the generals and the politicians. Montgomery's Memoirs do not give one the impression that things were at all bad in this respect.

They were bad in World War One, and, in my experience, good in World War Two. One reason was that the set-up in World War Two, with a Minister of Defence, a Defence Committee of the Cabinet on which the Chiefs of Staff sat, was much superior to the methods obtaining in World War One. Another was, of course, the personality of Sir Winston Churchill. A further reason, I think, was that when we went into World War One no one in the Cabinet except Sir Winston Churchill had actual experience of war. In World War Two, many of us in the Government had fought in World War One. We knew what phrases like 'If necessary, switch the attack to ...' meant in terms of bloodshed and miles of mud struggled through. And, of course, the generals in World War Two had been in the trenches in World War One as well.

I think the relations between politicians and the military in this country are usually good, and that we have plenty we can teach any other country you care to name. Montgomery has made some speeches which have caused a bit of trouble, but I don't think this in any way means that he doesn't have a proper understanding, or regard, for the relation of the soldier to the statesman. It is simply that he is the kind of chap who puts his foot in it from time to time, partly because he gets things wrong occasionally, partly because he is an outspoken fellow, and partly because, even at seventy, he is still something of the naughty boy.

The Need for Discussion

Another question, of course, is whether generals should publish books so soon after the battles are over. Accounts which, though written in good faith, may be inaccurate, or at least highly subjective, can damage international relations. I am all for people being candid about international relations, when we can be sure that it is facts and not debatable versions of facts that we are being candid about. It can't be very pleasant for wives and mothers to hear that though their husbands and sons did not die in vain, they might not have died at all if two generals could have agreed about a particular plan.

A flourishing democracy, anxious to learn from its own mistakes as quickly as possible, so that it can be stronger and happier, needs to get the discussion of vital controversy going as quickly as possible after the event; but in my view books of this kind are coming out too soon after the event for democracy to be able to record a balance of advantages therefrom.

One thing that I particularly like and admire about Montgomery is that in spite of his histrionics, naughtiness, and occasional irresponsibilities, he is in the last analysis a serious person. He may think a great deal about himself, but he thinks, too, a great deal about leadership in a free society. Like the great captains of history, he understands that in the last ditch the sanction of the true leader is a moral one – he leads by the moral example he sets his men, in terms of courage, integrity and steadfastness of purpose. I admire the role that he makes virtue, however defined, play in his personal and public life.

Dynamic Force is Leadership

One of the valuable contributions that this book may make to contemporary society is to remind people that techniques and organisation, whether military or civil, are ultimately of secondary importance: the dynamic force is leadership – at all levels – and the leader's power is not know-how but the capacity to command the respect of ordinary men. Leadership, I agree with Montgomery, depends ultimately on character.

Montgomery's Memoirs have the stamp of Montgomery on every page. Outspoken, trenchant, speaking in language which everybody can understand, he says what he means, and says it bluntly. It is a big book, because he is a big man. If it is not always accurate, and not always judicious, it is always stirring and sincere, as its author always is. Many may think less of him as a judge of men and affairs after they have read it; but nobody will think the less of Montgomery as a man.

11
George Lansbury: Man of His Day

A hundred years ago to-morrow in a toll house in Suffolk there was born George Lansbury, destined to become one of the best known and most colourful of Labour leaders. His father was a hard-drinking navvy, and it was the peripatetic nature of his calling which caused his son to be born a countryman. After sundry vicissitudes the family eventually settled in East London, and Lansbury grew up to be a typical East Londoner, though in outward appearance he might well have passed for a country farmer with his powerful physique, side whiskers, and his bowler hat always slightly on one side.

His schooling was scrappy for it was before the days of compulsory education. He had various jobs before settling down to the heavy work as a contractor in the coal trade.

Late Victorian

It was in the noisy, rather rough, and drunken environment of Stepney in the latter part of Queen Victoria's reign that his character was formed. He became a strong teetotaller. He experienced religion when young and, although for a few years he was an agnostic, for most of his life he was a fervent Christian and a member of the Church of England. He took an early interest in politics, hearing Gladstone and other orators at meetings and attending frequently in the gallery of the House of Commons, where he heard some of the famous Home Rule debates.

Life in East London though rough was cheerful and Lansbury always had a certain cheerful noisiness and had a tendency to shout in his speeches, which were frequently emotional. Ramsay MacDonald did not like him, calling him to me 'that noisy fellow,' while the *Morning Post* in later years described him as 'that rampageous old Socialist.'

He was indeed a bit rampageous.

Here in East London he found his life partner, Elizabeth Brine, with whom he enjoyed so many happy years and who bore him 12 children. In 1884, lured by specious advertisements, he tried his luck by emigrating to Australia, but found the prospects very different from what had been held out to him, and returned home after a year. He retained always a strong interest in Britain oversea and later in the House of Commons founded a group in the Labour Party to study colonial and imperial problems. On his return he found work in his father-in-law's saw mill, and after his death succeeded to the business, which he carried on successfully.

A keen reformer, he naturally joined the Liberal Party, but gradually became disillusioned by Gladstone's indifference to social reform and by the aridity of John Morley. He continued to work in the Liberal Party up to the 1895 election, but became increasingly drawn to Socialism. He got to know William Morris, Hyndman, and other Socialist leaders and was for some time active in the Social Democratic Federation, even fighting a propaganda fight in Walworth under their auspices, but he was no materialist Marxian and his natural political home was the Independent Labour Party, in which body were many Christian Socialists. He was also a keen trade unionist and it was as a trade union nominee that he first got into Parliament.

A New Force

During the last years of the nineteenth and the first decade of the twentieth century while working at his business his weekends were occupied with meetings all over the country and he became known as one of the most forcible speakers on Socialist platforms. Political meetings were then far more popular than they are today and the hundreds of meetings every weekend up and down the country were instrumental in building up the Labour Party as a new force in politics. Lansbury's magnificent physique enabled him to undertake a tremendous programme while his passionate sincerity had a great effect. Meanwhile he engaged in local political work in Poplar, for he had now settled with his large family in Bow. He became a borough councillor and a Poor Law Guardian. Under the leadership of Will Crooks and himself Poplar became the advanced guard in London Labour.

Sixty years ago there were still British Socialists who believed that the social revolution would come about by force. The Paris commune and the barricades were still a living memory, but Lansbury, a convinced pacifist, believed in constitutional change and in democratic methods. Nevertheless, he twice took action which involved conflict with authority. The Poor Law, especially in East London, was administered on the harsh principles of 1834, but Lansbury, Crooks, and the other Labour guardians in Poplar persuaded their colleagues to treat people as human beings and not as paupers. Authority intervened and an inquiry into Poplar administration was set on foot by the Local Government Board. Wild accusations of corruption were made, but Lansbury and his colleagues were completely cleared, while the revelations of Poor Law methods were partly instrumental in causing the Royal Commission on the Poor Law to be set up. Nevertheless, a good deal of the mud stuck and Poplarism became a term of abuse.

Lansbury served on the Royal Commission and was one of the signatories with Mrs. Sidney Webb of the Minority report, the principles of which, in the course of years, were adopted and brought to an end the old Poor Law. The practical demonstration of what could be done in this field played as big a part in reform as the more theoretical work of the Webbs.

The other occasion was after the First World War when in protest against the unequal burden of the rates in London the Poplar Labour Councillors led by Lansbury and Miss Susan Lawrence went to prison for refusing to levy a rate for the precept of the Greater London local authorities. Here again the protest was effective and an equalization of rates measure for London was passed into law.

In Parliament

After several unsuccessful attempts Lansbury was elected to Parliament for Bow and Bromley in 1910 but with characteristic devotion to principle he resigned his seat in order to fight as a Woman's Suffrage candidate but was defeated and did not re-enter the House of Commons until 1922. Lansbury was generally inclined to take a left-wing line and did not submit easily to party discipline. He was not included in the 1924 Labour Government but was made First Commissioner of Works in that of 1929.

Lansbury was by many people set down as a mere sentimentalist, all heart and no head, but this was a mistake. He was a good business man. He was not an advocate of giving public money away indiscriminately and was a sound municipal administrator. In the face of enormous difficulties he managed to found and run the first successful Labour daily paper, the *Daily Herald*, until eventually it was taken over as the official organ of the Party.

In office he was a great success and Londoners still profit by his enlightened policy. Breaking through old-fashioned views he threw open the Royal Parks for games and established the swimming pool known as Lansbury's Lido by the Serpentine. I have no doubt that had he had the chance in other offices he would have shown the same practical imaginativeness.

Holding the views he did, it was natural that Lansbury should have opposed strongly the action of MacDonald in 1931. In the General Election of that year Lansbury was the only ex-Cabinet minister to be returned in the little band of survivors of the storm. Lansbury, like Keir Hardie, did not really enjoy Parliamentary life. Although he held many offices in the party, his natural bent was to independent action. He was a prophet and a preacher rather than a Parliamentarian. However, he took on the burden of leadership in the House of Commons at the age of 72. He inspired and led for four years a little party of 45, many of whom were past doing much work, and made it into an effective opposition. During that time Lansbury, Stafford Cripps, and I shared the opposition leader's room and one or other of us was always on the Front Bench.

Ablest Leader

Day after day the work had to be allocated to the members. Lansbury was successful in inspiring and leading this little band, thus, as Mr. Baldwin said at the time, saving Parliamentary Government. A Labour member once said to a Conservative Whip: 'I think G. L. is the best man I have ever known.' To which the Whip replied: 'Best, is that all? He's the ablest leader of the opposition I have ever seen.'

Lansbury's position was made increasingly difficult by the course of international events. Brought up in the safe Victorian days, he was a convinced Christian Pacifist and bitterly opposed all war and armaments. As the world situation got tenser he found it difficult to be leader of a party which had accepted Arthur Henderson's policy of collective security. Hating cruelty and dictatorship he could not bring himself to accept the need for force to oppose them. This led to his resignation of the leadership of the party, to the great regret of his colleagues who while unable to accept his views had immense affection and respect for him. Lansbury was entirely free from the pharisaic intolerance of some pacifists. He willingly recognized the sincerity of those who could not agree with him. I worked in the closest contact with him for many years and although we disagreed, I do not think that we ever quarrelled.

The last years of his life were devoted to a pathetic effort to try by sweet reasonableness to convince toughs such as Hitler and Mussolini to see the error of their ways. He died in 1940 before he could see the destruction by bombing of the East London he had lived in and loved for so many years.

George Lansbury was a man of his time. He had the moral earnestness of the Victorians. It was not for him to plan in detail the New Jerusalem, but by example as well as precept to show people the way of life which they must follow if a new society was to be built on firm foundations. He preached love of one's fellow men and practised it himself. He received in abundance the love of those who worked with him.

12
Mr. Churchill's Eden

Mr. Randolph Churchill tells us in his preface that he agreed to write this book* just before Nasser nationalised the Suez Canal. It was to have been a simple success story. It then became a tragedy. The successful politician undertook the Suez adventure, became gravely ill and retired from political life.

This, Mr. Churchill says, affected the way in which he has told his story. It would be interesting to speculate on what he would have written if these unhappy events had not occurred. Would he have come to praise Anthony or to bury him? It appears that, long before Suez, Mr. Churchill had made up his mind that his father's blue-eyed boy was not up to the position for which he was being groomed.

The book is in fact an essay in the art of denigration. It is not in any way a biography, for there is little or no evidence of serious research. A few pages dismiss Sir Anthony's early life and upbringing. He is allowed to be good-looking, charming and brave, but these qualities are mentioned mainly in order to emphasise the lack of others.

In Detail

A typical instance is his reference to Sir Anthony's maiden speech in the House of Commons. Mr. Churchill makes use of it to inform us that it is believed that he wrote it himself, whereas in later life most of his speeches were ghost-written for him. He adds that the careful choice of cliché, the avoidance of anything even

The Rise and Fall of Sir Anthony Eden by Randolph Churchill. MacGibbon and Kee, 1959.

bordering on the controversial and of any original thought or phrase, seem to have been noted by those who drafted his speeches fifteen and twenty years later. The author spends two and a half pages on detailing Sir Anthony's oratorical deficiencies with a gusto equalled only when he explains that Eden's rise was by calculated subservience to Mr. Baldwin.

Much of the book is taken up with Mr. Churchill's own account of the political history of the years between the wars. This has been done better by other hands. Our author is not very well informed. He should surely know that the late Mr. William Graham did not support Mr. MacDonald in the 1931 crisis, but was one of his stoutest opponents, for which he earned the bitter hatred of Philip Snowden. But accuracy is not one of Mr. Churchill's strong points. In detailing the group of Conservatives who became out of sympathy with the Chamberlain Government, he gets two Christian names wrong out of twelve. A small matter, but indicative of carelessness.

The main purpose of the detailed history of the lamentable record of the Tory Government prior to the Second World War is to make it clear that for much of the time Sir Anthony was as much an accomplice as the chief villains of the piece: Halifax, Hoare, Chamberlain and Simon. This is designed to belittle Sir Anthony's courage in resigning over the policy of the Chamberlain Government in respect of Mussolini. Mr. Churchill makes it clear that he regards Eden as one of the guilty men. He cannot understand why he did not resign earlier. Curiously enough, he does not pass the same strictures on Lord Norwich, better known as Mr. Duff Cooper, who resigned later than Eden – but then Mr. Churchill admired Duff Cooper.

Low Estimate

It would appear that Sir Winston did not share his son's views, for while he got rid of most of the adherents of Chamberlain, he not only retained Eden but made him heir apparent. One would gather from this book that Sir Winston was deceived by Eden's successful visit to Cairo in October, 1940, into thinking that Eden was a bigger man than he was. I don't think it likely. Indeed, the passage quoted from Sir Winston, one of many used to pad out the narrative, proves it.

It is quite clear that Sir Winston did not share the low estimate of Eden that his son held. He designated him as his successor and his choice was accepted by the Conservative Party. There is a story of an indifferent speaker who was imported into a western city in America. As his speech proceeded he was alarmed to see many of the audience producing six-shooters. He was, however, reassured when he was told that they were not gunning for him but for the man who was responsible for bringing him there. Mr. Randolph Churchill should have thought of that before writing this book.

Different Story

In dealing with the short and unhappy reign of Sir Anthony at Downing Street, our author begins by criticising him for not having remade the Government according to his own taste. One gathers that his father's Administration was full of junk. He appears not to have consulted our author. It is interesting that Mr. Churchill recognises that, for the past four years, Britain's economic situation had been deteriorating. This is rather different from the usual Conservative success story.

The curious incident of the frogman, Commander Crabb, and the Russian cruiser is used to show that Sir Anthony failed to keep in proper touch with the secret service; while apparently the dismissal of Glubb Pasha should have been met by drastic action despite the advice of Glubb himself.

The latter part of the book is taken up with an examination of the Suez incident. (This is the part which was serialised in the *Daily Express.*) I think Mr. Churchill is fully justified in his strictures on the policy and actions of the Government. I understand that his account of the operation is substantially correct. I have never been able to understand why Sir Anthony embarked on a policy which ran counter to all the principles on which his political reputation had been founded and I shall read with interest his own account when his book is published. Not much light on this is thrown by Mr. Churchill. He frankly confesses that his first opinions on the venture have had to be revised, and he quotes with great effect his grandfather's denunciation of Gladstone's action at the time of the Arab revolt.

Cloud of Suez

Sir Anthony's health broke down and he resigned under the cloud of the Suez colossal blunder and was succeeded by the present Prime Minister. In dealing with the inter-war period Mr. Churchill emphasises the importance of the collective responsibility of the Cabinet in order to make Eden as responsible as Chamberlain, Simon and the rest for policies of the Conservative Government of that time. Sir Anthony must clearly bear a heavy share of the blame for Suez. What of his colleagues? Surely Mr. Churchill must feel that Messrs. Macmillan, Butler and Lloyd must share the burden with him? No, Mr. Churchill was prepared to offer himself to the electors of Bournemouth as a loyal supporter of Mr. Macmillan as against the peccant Mr. Nigel Nicolson.

Biographies not infrequently reveal more of the character of the author than the subject. Readers of this book will not learn much about Sir Anthony Eden, but they should get a full appreciation of Mr. Randolph Churchill.

13
From Victorian to Elizabethan
The Role of the Monarchy

I have been active in the Socialist movement for more than half a century. During that period I have taken part in bringing about a number of changes in British society.

Some old established things, such as the Poor Law, I have helped to abolish, but there is one feature of it which I have never felt any urge to abolish, and that is the monarchy. I have never been a republican even in theory, and certainly not in practice.

The Labour Party has never been republican. British Socialists, with their own experiences of the long reign of Queen Victoria, differ from their Continental colleagues, with their memories of Habsburgs, Hohenzollerns and Bourbons. With that practical attitude which distinguishes them they have concentrated on the points which seemed most vital.

I remember Jimmie Maxton quoting John Wheatley as saying that he saw no point in substituting a bourgeois president for a bourgeois king. The republicanism which attracted middle-class politicians like Joseph Chamberlain in the 1870s had lost its attractive force by the time the Socialist movement began to gather strength. Capitalism, not monarchy, was the enemy.

Relish with Their Tea

Furthermore, the main influence in the Labour movement has been working class not middle class. The workers had not that feeling of inferiority which was found often in the nineteenth-century bourgeois. To-day you will find the greatest enthusiasm for the monarch in the meanest streets. Somehow they feel an affinity.

I remember a boy in my Limehouse club saying: 'Some people say as how the King and Queen are different from us. They aren't. The only difference is that they can have a relish with their tea every day.'

The advantage of constitutional kingship is, in my view, very simple. The monarch is the general representative of all the people and stands aloof from the party political battle. A president, however popular, is bound to have been chosen as representative of some political trend, and as such is open to attack from those of a different view. A monarch is a kind of referee, although the occasions when he or she has to blow the whistle are nowadays very few.

The monarchy attracts to itself the kind of sentimental loyalty which otherwise might go to the leader of a faction. There is, therefore, far less danger under a constitutional monarchy of the people being carried away by a Hitler, a Mussolini or even a de Gaulle. The monarchy gives a certain stability and continuity to the government. The substitution of one political leader for another causes no upset. The Queen's Government is carried on. The institution was not seriously affected even by the abdication of King Edward VIII, which elsewhere might have caused very serious trouble.

A King Every Four Years

The most stable and successful republic is that of the United States of America, and Americans are currently supposed to be most critical of what they call 'this King business.' Yet America is really more monarchical than Britain.

In effect, what they do is to elect a king for a period of four years. The powers of the President are much the same as those enjoyed by our King William III. What he does with those powers depends largely on his personal will. There is all the difference in the world between a Roosevelt and a Coolidge, just as there was between a Henry III and an Edward I.

There is the serious disadvantage of combining in one person the symbol of the nation and the party leader. The point is well illustrated by the story of a British general dining with his

American opposite number. At the end of dinner the British general rose, glass in hand, and gave 'The Queen,' adding 'God bless her.' He then gave 'The President of the United States.' The President was a Democrat. The American general, a Republican, said 'The President,' and added 'God help us.'

A British king making himself a dictator is unthinkable, but many thoughtful Americans would not deny that a President might do so.

However, even though Americans criticise monarchy as an institution, you would go a long way to find Americans who would criticise the British monarchy in practice. Our late King was much admired in the United States, so is our present Queen. The same is true of the attitude of the French people to them.

Common Symbol of Unity

One may ask here whether it is the institution or the monarchs who have maintained it in being. Britain has been well served by its last three monarchs, but it is noteworthy also that the greatest progress towards the democratic Socialism in which I believe has been made not in republics but in limited monarchies.

Norway, Sweden and Denmark are probably the three countries where there is the highest degree of equality of well-being. They, like Britain, have been fortunate in having monarchs who are democratic and imbued with the spirit of service, while the leading statesmen have been, and are, practical men who understand the needs of their people and are tolerant. It may be said that in all these countries the persons have flattered the institution.

There is one other very practical point in favour of monarchy. The British Commonwealth is made up of a great variety of peoples. More and more they need a common symbol of unity. Some of these peoples are inheritors to a high degree of the sentiment of loyalty to the monarch; others have this to a lesser degree. Yet others are now republics, but the monarch is there as head of the Commonwealth, a living symbol of unity which cannot be replaced by a formula, still less by a president elected by all the constituent peoples of the Commonwealth.

Though I saw Queen Victoria and King Edward VII, the first monarch that I actually met was King George V. He was an excellent King. He was not, I think, a man of unusual intelligence nor, I should judge, as able as his father or his successor, but observant, hardworking, sympathetic, with a capacity for moving with the times even though this movement was not very much to his taste.

In a modern democratic monarchy there is no reason why the monarch should be a genius. What is needed is a good, ordinary man who understands how to fill an extraordinary position.

War Experience in the Navy

I met George V only a few times, chiefly when I was Postmaster-General. He was a very fair-minded man, as those who have read what he had to say about his first encounter with Ramsay MacDonald when he came to form the first Labour Government will know. I don't think that there could be better testimony to the fair-mindedness and objectivity with which British monarchs of the twentieth century have viewed their functions than some of the jottings in George V's diary at this time. Very much on the theme 'they are Socialists, I know, but they must have their chance,' accompanied by references to the 'straightforwardness' and other qualities displayed by MacDonald personally.

George V had a very high sense of duty and his character was tested not only by the strain of the First World War but also by the constitutional crisis which arose over the House of Lords. George VI's sense of duty was even higher and was perhaps more informed and emanated from a more sensitive mind. He had to face a more perilous war and also changes at home and in the Commonwealth which required a high degree of adaptability, tolerance and historical insight.

No one could be in contact with him without realising his resolution to live up to the highest ideals of kingship. Without losing dignity he had the common touch. Like his father, he had the advantage of not having begun life as the heir to the throne and of having served in the Navy – and not only in peacetime.

I suppose that if he had had the choice, George VI would have preferred the life of a country gentleman interested in farming and in field sports. Naturally his immediate entourage was drawn from people of similar tastes who would normally be Conservatives. I should think that his own outlook was that of a broadminded Conservative, but his range of information and interests was much wider than that of a country squire.

Understood Need for Change

He had a real knowledge of industry and understood the mind of the working people very well. His interest in the Industrial Welfare Society had taught him much. He understood the need for change. Thus, although he almost certainly disliked the idea of nationalisation he had no sympathy with the old type of employer and recognised that in the instance of the coal industry nationalisation was the only thing that held out hope for the miners.

His work with his boys' camps gave me a certain common ground, for this kind of work had also been one of my interests. This perhaps mitigated my lack of experience in his other activities.

All monarchs, provided that they are prepared to listen, acquire over the years a considerable stock of knowledge of men and affairs and if they have good judgment can give good advice acquired from the wide contacts which they have made. I imagine, too, that they are much helped by their private secretaries, who are generally men of high calibre. Certainly King George was fortunate in having Sir Alan Lascelles, who was, I think, an outstanding success in this difficult position. As well as ability, it requires infinite tact.

King George VI was supported most admirably by his gracious consort and undoubtedly one of the things which has strengthened the monarchy has been the picture of family life seen in the Royal Family. I remember saying one day to Mr. Nehru that the Royal Family was just the kind of symbol the Commonwealth needed because it appealed to all the various people composing it. We are fortunate, too, in having such a charming lady as our present Queen and her consort, the Duke of Edinburgh. They carry on to admiration a great tradition.

I remember being a little anxious when I was Prime Minister as to where a suitable consort would be found. I thought, 'Well, at any rate, the war has probably put an end to the possibility of her having to marry some stiff, German princeling.' One day I was dining with the Mountbattens and was introduced to a young man who impressed me by his obvious ability and charm, and it was with great pleasure that I learned of the engagement. Thank goodness the days of marriages for high political reasons have passed away.

A Chair and Cigarette

Reading the lives of my predecessors I have often thought how fortunate I was to have to deal with a George VI and not with a George IV or even Queen Victoria. I am struck by the difference between the stiffness and formality of the past and the ease of the present relations between the monarch and his chief adviser. I gather that Queen Victoria expected her Prime Minister to stand during an audience, whereas now he comes in and is invited to sit down and have a cigarette.

The conversation, too, was, I think, very formal. Queen Victoria may have unbent a bit to Dizzie, but not to Gladstone. I cannot imagine her saying to Lord Salisbury, for instance, 'How is Joe getting on with the Colonies?' but it would have been quite natural for George VI to say to me, 'How is Mannie hitting it off with the French generals?' or 'Well, Nye seems to be getting the doctors into line.' I, on the other hand, might have said to the King, 'The Old Man was really rather naughty in the House yesterday about India.'

At a private audience one does not nowadays have constantly to say 'Your Majesty.' 'Sir' is quite enough. Records in diaries or memoranda reproduced by official biographers sometimes seem rather bald, but actually these interviews are carried on in an atmosphere of informality, candid and friendly.

Incident at First Audience

In the pages of Sir John Wheeler-Bennett's admirable biography of King George VI the reader will come across a number of references to the audiences granted to me when I was Prime Minister. These are of course, the occasions when the Prime Minister is acting as Chief Minister and adviser of the monarch. Among the constitutional powers are those of encouraging, advising and warning.

Queen Victoria did not interpret her powers so narrowly. She would insist on a particular person being made Foreign Secretary while she laid an absolute ban on the appointment of Labouchere as a Minister. Under King George VI the constitutional theory became an actuality. King George never raised objection to any appointment.

The official biography makes rather too much of an incident which occurred at my first audience after becoming Prime Minister in 1945. I had to form a Ministry in a very short time owing to having to get back to Potsdam. All I could do was to fill the most important offices.

When I saw the King I had not come to a definite conclusion on the question as to the positions of Foreign Secretary and Chancellor of the Exchequer. The choice lay between Mr. Dalton and Mr. Bevin. Both were qualified for either post. I was at first inclined to put Mr. Dalton at the Foreign Office – as he had been Under-Secretary in 1929 – and make Mr. Bevin Chancellor, since he had served on the Macmillan Committee and was well versed in finance. I don't recollect that the King expressed any very strong views on the subject, but he seemed inclined to prefer Mr. Bevin as Foreign Secretary.

Not a Decisive Factor

After the audience I reconsidered the matter and decided that it would be better to put Mr. Bevin at the Foreign Office. There were various reasons for this, one of which was that a very important and able man, Mr. Morrison, who was going to co-ordinate home matters did not get on very well with Mr. Bevin. As Chancellor of the Exchequer Mr. Bevin would have been constantly in contact with Mr. Morrison, which might have led to friction on quite minor matters. It therefore seemed wiser to give these two leading members of the Government spheres of action where there was not so much opportunity for a clash of personalities. I naturally took into account the King's view, which was very sound; but it was not a decisive factor in my arrival at my decision.

The only other occasion on which Sir John Wheeler-Bennett reports the King as intervening was over the Supplies and Services Bill, which we passed in the emergency session when we were faced with a financial crisis. The King felt that I had not explained the matter sufficiently. The King was under the impression that we were seeking dictatorial powers which might have justified the 'Police State' stunt which Sir Winston had tried to run in the 1945 election.

The introduction of this Bill encouraged Sir Winston to revive this old cry. King George was deceived into thinking that there was substance in it. He became quite happy again when he realised that this was only an Opposition stunt and that there was in fact no basis for any anxiety.

The two principal constitutional powers remaining to the Crown are the selection of the person to whom a commission to form a new Administration should be entrusted and the granting or refusing a dissolution to a Prime Minister.

The first did not cause any trouble in my case as I had been returned as the Leader of a big majority. However, when the first meeting of the Parliamentary Labour Party after the new Parliament had assembled took place, it would have been open to the party to turn me down as leader. In that case I should have had to return to the King saying that I could not form a Government and he would have had to send for someone else.

There are several instances in the nineteenth century of the man sent for having to return his commission. Recently the Queen had to decide on the person to form a new administration on the resignation of Sir Anthony Eden. Here is an instance where the monarch, after seeking such advice as he or she chooses, makes a personal decision as to whom to send for.

Choosing Time to Dissolve

It is rare now for a request by a Prime Minister for a dissolution to be refused, though there was a case in Canada where Lord Byng, the Governor-General, the representative of the Crown, refused to give one to Mr. Mackenzie King. It might well have arisen had the Labour Government been defeated in the House of Commons when there was only a majority of six. The King would have been within his rights in sending for the Leader of the Opposition if he thought that a working majority in the House could have been obtained by him. King George V might, had he chosen, have refused a dissolution to Ramsay MacDonald in 1924, but I fancy it was thought impolitic to refuse the request of the first Labour Prime Minister.

The choice of the time to dissolve is one for the Prime Minister. I had to make such a decision in 1951. The official biography of King George VI might give the impression that I was pushed into going to the country by some pressure from the King. There is no substance in this, but the position of the King was one which I personally had to take into account.

There was then no apprehension of the King's death, but he was about to make an extensive journey to Australia and New Zealand. His health was not good and owing to his extreme conscientiousness he was apt to worry.

We had a majority of only six in the House of Commons. We had some elderly and ailing Members. There was always the possibility of defeat, as we depended on the precarious health of our own Members and the unpredictable actions of the handful of Liberals. I did not think it fair to let the King depart with this constant worry of a possible political crisis hanging over him.

There were, of course, other reasons for seeking an election. Strongest of all was the almost unbearable strain on our Members, but, I think rightly, the position of the King had to be given due weight.

In my view, Britain has been very fortunate in having monarchs who understand how to function in a democratic society and will act accordingly. I never knew King George VI to do anything that was not constitutionally correct. Under him the British monarchy increased its popularity and its prestige.

14

The Hiroshima Choice

In a book recently published in the United States, written by Mr. Michael Amrine and entitled *The Great Decision**, the author professes to give the secret history of the atomic bomb. In fact it does not add much to our knowledge. There are full accounts of discussions between President Truman and his civilian and military colleagues and with the scientists. The pros and cons of the problem are set out and the reasons given for the decision. It was one of the curious things in history that when the time arrived for using this new instrument of war, the political heads of the two countries concerned, the United States and the United Kingdom, were both new to the job.

In the Dark

Mr. Truman, despite the obvious possibility of his having to take over power at short notice, had been kept completely out of the picture by President Roosevelt. All he knew was that money was being spent on some secret project.

I myself was aware of the project. I knew it was a race between the Germans and the Allies for the production of a super-bomb, for we had had to take steps to sabotage the heavy water installation in Norway which was part of the plant for making atomic energy, but further knowledge of the subject was confined to a very limited circle. All I knew was that Tube Alloys was the name for the work being done on this project under the general supervision of Sir John Anderson, but the first news I had of it

*Putnam's, New York, 1959.

was from President Truman at Potsdam, when he told me of the successful explosion in New Mexico.

Agreement for the dropping of the bomb by the United States had already been given by Sir Winston Churchill on behalf of Britain. I was, therefore, not called upon to make a decision, but if I had been I should have agreed with President Truman, for the facts relevant to the decision before us at the time were these.

The Japanese, despite heavy bombing attacks on their homeland, showed no signs of giving way. Our experts considered that they could hold out for another six months. There were Japanese forces scattered widely throughout South-East Asia. We well knew their fanatical loyalty and that they preferred death to surrender. To hunt them all out would have been very costly in lives on both sides, as would a projected invasion of the mainland.

We now possessed a bomb infinitely more powerful than any hitherto produced. There was a hope that either by threat of using, or by actual demonstration, the war would be brought to a rapid conclusion. If the bomb had to be used, it would mean the destruction of one or two great cities, with a loss of life that might run into a hundred thousand. Six months more war might mean a million deaths or more.

President Truman consulted his military advisers, one of whom seems to have had scruples on the ground that it was ungentlemanly warfare, a rather delayed qualm after what had been done by orthodox bombing, but the majority of his advisers, civil and military, agreed that the bomb should be used. His was the decision and courageously he took it.

Proper Question

The really curious part of the story is that steps were taken to find out, by means of a questionaire, what were the views of the scientists and technicians. This is as if I should ask the makers of my motor-car the best road to York.

The proper question to have been put to them was: 'What is the immediate effect of the bomb and are there any after-effects?' I knew nothing whatever about the genetic effects of an atomic explosion! I knew nothing about fall-out and all the rest of what emerged after Hiroshima. As far as I know, President Truman, Sir

Winston Churchill and Sir John Anderson knew nothing of these things. Did the scientists? If so, did they warn the President? Or did they not know about the long-range effects of atom-splitting?

This book is full of hindsight talk about the new atomic age, but these questions are not answered or even raised.

15

An American 'Statesman of the Century'

If I had to name the six greatest American statesmen of the twentieth century, I would certainly include George Marshall.

The two Roosevelts, Wilson, MacArthur and Truman are all much better known than he is, being both more prominent on the field of politics and more colourful by nature. Intellectually, however, he was inferior to none of them, and their equal in human wisdom and political judgment. Judged as a moral being, he may have been the greatest of them, his wonderful self-control, gentleness and courtesy weighing the balance in his favour.

Much of what I admired about George Marshall came my way through what I learned about him from Harry Truman. Truman – a born democrat, with no illusions about anybody, but a respect for all, and not at all disposed to consider anybody his superior – frankly looked up to Marshall. He admired his capacity for devotion – to his wife, to his friends, to his country.

Two Great Gifts

Truman, a good judge of dutifulness, thought Marshall the most dedicated man he ever met. His praise for him as a soldier-statesman was of the highest.

As a soldier, Marshall had two gifts which amounted to genius. To be really great a general must prove himself a trainer of troops. Marshall raised an army of millions out of a few thousands. Whatever training could do for a host untried in war, Marshall's training did.

Secondly, a general must be able to choose his subordinate commanders. Eisenhower, Patton and Bradley were three quite different types. Each with totally different contributions to make, but each in his way wonderfully suited for the role Marshall required him to take. They were a pretty formidable trio between them, and it was Marshall who raised them and kept them in harness.

Man of Calibre

My first acquaintance with Marshall was when he arrived in this country with Harry Hopkins just after the Americans had entered the war, in order to find out exactly what we were up to, and to tell us how Americans thought things should be done. I think that references to 'presence' and 'personal greatness' are frequently misplaced, and often misleading, but it is a matter of fact that one could not spend more than a few minutes with Marshall before coming to the conclusion that here was a man of calibre. He was an excellent listener, and when he eventually spoke he made an impression of open-mindedness and objectivity.

The first thing he had to tell us, of course, was that the Americans wanted to 'wade in' in Europe. We had to tell him why we were against it. It could not have been an easy thing for him to sit and learn from us. Only a man of Marshall's stamp could have done it, and learned so quickly. In grasping the total situation as quickly as he did, Marshall performed a great service to his country, and to the West.

Understood British

I always felt that Marshall understood us in this country better than any other American general, and, indeed, much better than many American statesmen. Perhaps his objective aim was helped in this respect by his being a Virginian.

I have always felt, especially during my visits to the United States, that there is a peculiar affinity between us and the citizens of the Southern States. Politically, they are often very much to the right of us. But emotionally and culturally, in a curious kind of way, they are often nearer to us than other Americans who politically and intellectually have more in common with us. I think many other people over here shared my view about him, and it stood us in great stead at those times when inevitably we and the Americans were having some difficulty in coming to agreement.

It has sometimes occurred to me that George Marshall resembled the best of our British generals more than he did some of his best American colleagues. De Tocqueville says in 'Democracy in America' that American generals tend to be the way they are because they are full-time professional soldiers with no other status and security in society than they can earn in their profession.

China Mission

He contrasts the tendency they sometimes display to restlessness, ambition and political activity with the more or less indifferent attitude to politics displayed by generals who were peers and landowners and went into battle only because it was thought that *noblesse oblige*. He even suggests that American officers had a tendency to favour warfare as the state of affairs in which they were most likely to be promoted and thus earn social status.

De Tocqueville was writing more than a hundred years ago, but there may be something still in what he says. At any rate, Marshall, with his Virginian background, his political disinterestedness, his repugnance towards warfare, and his aristocratic bearing and cast of mind, brings de Tocqueville's saying back to mind.

Marshall's intellectual acumen, and again his capacity for being objective, were best shown, I think, in the report he made on the situation in China when he went there on a special mission for President Truman in 1946. President Truman tells an interesting little anecdote about this. When he decided that somebody had better go to China and see exactly what was going on, he thought that Marshall was the man for the job. Marshall had just retired from his post as Chief of Staff of the Army.

Truman rang the General at his home in Leesburg, and when he heard the General's voice, said: 'General, I want you to go to China for me.' Marshall replied, 'Yes, Mr. President,' and then replaced the receiver.

Truman thought that a bit odd at the time, and asked Marshall

when he came to the White House two days later why he had
hung up so abruptly. Marshall apologised and said that he and
Mrs. Marshall had only just arrived at the house in which they
were to spend his retirement when the phone rang. He had not
wanted Mrs. Marshall, who was concerned about his health, to
know how short-lived his retirement was going to be. He had put
the phone down so that she would not hear, hoping to break it to
her gradually.

Warm Conviction

His report on China was a model of objectivity. Objectivity is
difficult to achieve even in the most favourable circumstances.
Marshall wrote a cool analysis of the situation between Chiang
Kai-shek and the Communists at a time when this was the hottest
issue in American domestic politics.

Objectivity, too, is often the product of a somewhat cold and
disengaged nature. There was nothing cold or disengaged about
Marshall, as anybody who ever had conversation with him, or
heard him giving testimony before a Congressional Committee,
will know. He was a man of warmth and conviction. And that
was why his impartial views on any situation commanded an
attention which those of the cold fish never got.

If anything could have got Chiang's fortunes back into shape it
was Marshall's advice. Truman blames the loss of China on
Chiang's refusal to listen to Marshall. I think it was less due to
Chiang Kai-shek than to the hopeless feuding amongst the
families around him. They had the mentality of warlords, and the
day of the feudal warlord had long passed.

Marshall was very fortunate – though not more fortunate than
he deserved – to see one of the most bold, enlightened and good-
natured acts in the history of nations go on the record in
association with his name. Quite what share he had in the original
conception of the Marshall Plan I do not know. I see little point in
discussing it. The inspiration of the Marshall Plan was complex:
many people say that the key figure was Ernest Bevin, who acted
swiftly, before anybody else, on the implications of the famous
speech Marshall made at Harvard, and stubbornly hung on to
them until these implications were accepted somewhat bewilde-
redly by American policy-makers as an actuality.

The really important thing that Marshall did – and the Marshall Plan was only part of it – was to play an integral part in the process by which after the war the Americans were prevented from reverting to the isolationist attitude of mind from which even the great Wilson could not sever them in 1919. It would be interesting to discover just how much Marshall did in this respect. Certainly we know that he applied the full resources of his magnificent military reputation, his political disinterestedness and his widely admired personal character to warning the Americans against putting back the clock.

Roman Figure

The advocacy in influential circles in the United States of a great soldier turned out to be infinitely more influential than that of a great teacher. Generals have always exercised tremendous influence on public opinion in the United States – especially when they have refrained from going into politics.

However, it would not be fitting to pay tribute to the memory of Marshall by dwelling on those deeds of his which have already won the approbation of history. Marshall would not have cared much whether public opinion approved or disapproved of what he did, or whether he was generally thought a success or a failure. Duty was his god, and I am sure that what he would like to have had said about him, and the only thing, would be that he did his duty.

He always struck me as a curiously Roman figure, something of the type of a Roman general who flourished in the days of the Republic; something, perhaps, of a Cincinnatus, always ready to come out and fight, and once the duty was done, anxious to get back to the farm. When Americans are accused of producing 'political' generals, they can always retort with 'Marshall.'

16
Uncle Fred Looks Back

Just after the Second World War, I remember hearing Lord Woolton referred to as the father figure of the Conservative Party. An inappropriate description, in my view, because Fred Marquis's role always seemed essentially that of an uncle. He is as much Uncle Fred to the Conservatives as was the late Arthur Henderson Uncle Arthur to Labour.

Some achieve avuncularity, some have the avuncular role thrust upon them. Lord Woolton was a born uncle and this, I think, was the secret of the success he had with the post-war Conservative Party. Uncles, unlike fathers, combine authority with lack of power. A ticking off from an uncle one can take in one's stride: when uncle gives one half a crown, one feels no sense of obligation – that is what uncle is there for. So it was with Fred. He was influential and the Conservatives did what he told them to do. Yet somehow they never took him quite seriously. He was Carnot the organiser of victory, but Fred Karno all the same.

Work in Slums

It is not generally known that Lord Woolton started in life as a social reformer, which makes his account* of his early experiences very interesting. When he left the University, unable to become a Sociology research Fellow because he considered he could not afford it, he devoted his spare time to social work in the slums of Liverpool, later becoming head of what was virtually a university

*The Memoirs of the Rt. Hon. The Earl of Woolton, C.H., P.C. Cassell, 1959.

settlement, living in a mean street. 'Why are so many people poor?' became the dominating question in his consciousness.

The future organiser of the Conservative Party was then a member of the Fabian Society. He recalls meeting Keir Hardie at the house of a rich Liverpool socialist. After supper Hardie said to Fred Marquis privately: 'This is a very dangerous house for a young man to be in – I am a vegetarian, a teetotaller, a non-smoker, and I always sleep on a hard bed. I have reduced my wants to a minimum and no one can buy me.' Lord Woolton was, he tells us, much impressed by this very characteristic utterance. However, the need for changing his bed never arose.

Left the Fabians

When the 1914 war came his health did not allow him to join the Services, for his category was C-3. He was employed as an economist in the War Office. Here he found that he had great business ability. He supplied boots for the Russian and other Allied armies, blankets for the French and apparently the material for the building of the Murman railway. His experience in the War Office not unnaturally made him distrustful of bureaucracy. He dropped his membership of the Fabian Society and resolved never to get mixed up in politics.

There are many examples of successful business men turning in their mature years to philanthropy, but Lord Woolton is the only example of which I know of a social worker becoming a highly successful business man.

It must not be thought that Fred Marquis had abandoned his interest in the curing of the ills of poverty, but he believed in another way of curing them through the development of the retail trade and bringing cheap goods to the masses. After the war the enterprising and forward-looking Jewish firm of David Lewis, owners of a big multiple shop, took him on – on probation only, at his own request. Within two years he became a partner of this great business, and ultimately its chairman.

Prodigious Feat

When the Second World War broke out, Fred Marquis, though non-political, was well known to top Conservatives and was asked to advise the Army on textiles. There was a shortage at the time, but in four months he had solved the problem and had clothed the British Army, a prodigious feat. After that Neville Chamberlain asked him to be Minister of Food. This involved him in politics, for which he says he had little taste. But here again he did a first-class job, especially in making acceptable to the people the restrictions and rationing which the course of the war made essential.

He was a good colleague, but I was somewhat surprised when he undertook the job of chief Conservative organiser. He had often expressed criticism of the Tories to me and I had supposed that he was some kind of a Liberal. Perhaps he had also expressed his distrust of Labour men to the Tories, for as a salesman he had learnt the Pauline practice of being all things to all men.

The latter part of his book is less interesting. His career is well known and there is not much here to add to it. It reads rather like a Conservative Central Office pamphlet. There is one curious incident which throws some light on his attitude. When Neville Chamberlain asked him to become Minister of Food, he said that before saying anything he would have to consult his wife. Chamberlain expressed some surprise at this.

'This indeed surprised me,' says Woolton, 'and I asked him if he had any idea of the amount of the financial sacrifice that would be involved in my giving up my several and very lucrative business appointments.' When he consulted his wife about it, 'characteristically and with much wisdom her only reaction to this was "What does it matter."'

She was, of course, quite right, but what is odd is that such a thought should have occurred to Lord Woolton when so many of his fellow-countrymen were giving up not merely business appointments but life itself.

I don't for a moment suggest that Lord Woolton left the Fabian Society through self-interest. I think that he honestly believed that the way to the abolition of poverty was through business efficiency, a doctrine which naturally landed him in the Tory Party. I think that he had a natural habit of looking at things through rose-coloured spectacles. He thought things could be jollied along without too much friction. I think that there grew up with the years a veil between him and reality.

Beaming Britain

From a man of his prominence there is a curious reluctance to deal with matters of high importance. His only reference to public opinion apart from attacks on Labour policy is his disapproval of the American Loan. It would be interesting to know what he would have done if he had been still Minister of Food when the Americans turned off the tap of Lease-Lend at a moment's notice. There is hardly a reference to Foreign Affairs. There is nothing about the Korean War, and his narrative prudently stops short of the Suez adventure. The book ends with a picture of a beaming Britain reflecting the beaming face of Fred Woolton, with everything in the garden lovely except for these wicked Labour people.

Churchill's View

I do not think Lord Woolton much cared for Parliament. Big business men seldom do. That is why in wartime they get on fairly well – there is no real opposition – but in peacetime often turn out failures. They are not used to debate and they seldom understand the art of persuading a public assembly. In the wartime Government Lord Woolton, like Lord Leathers, did a first-class job as a departmental Minister, but after it, even in the sedate atmosphere of the House of Lords, neither was successful.

What would have happened to them in the Commons can hardly be contemplated. Lord Woolton is frank enough to record the opinion of Sir Winston Churchill on business men in politics. After a devastating massacre of the claims of the business men to be successful in politics, Winston wound up by saying: 'Surely, my dear Fred, you don't imagine the public look upon you as a business man. On the contrary, the public looks upon you as a great philanthropist.'

Precisely: a public uncle.

17

Jumping the Gun

Lord Alanbrooke, in my view, was one of the three great soldier-statesmen who emerged in World War II, ranking with the Americans Marshall – whom he much underestimates – and MacArthur – whom he somewhat overrates.

It is open to doubt whether Winston would have been the success he was if Alanbrooke had not been his Chief of the Imperial General Staff. If Alanbrooke had resigned under the strain so frequently manifested in his diaries, of which Volume II* has now appeared, his successor would almost certainly not have been able to strike the same precarious balance between the Prime Minister and the military men.

He would almost certainly have been too tough, or too weak, with Winston. In this case the delicately adjusted relationship would have disintegrated, incalculable damage would have been done to the Anglo-American alliance, the war indeed might have been lost. Britain and the West owe a debt to Alanbrooke.

I doubt, however, whether people will be more conscious of their debt to Alanbrooke, or readier to acknowledge it, as a result of the publication of this book.

Letting Public Know

Whether it is wise to publish diaries at all during the lifetime of their authors may be questioned. Lord Haig's reputation would

---

*Triumph In The West: 1943–1946, based on the diaries and auto-biographical notes of Field-Marshall Viscount Alanbrooke, K.G., O.M., by Arthur Bryant. Collins, 1959.

have stood far higher if his diary had never seen the light of day. The first volume of Alanbrooke was valuable because it revealed a great character for the first time, and gave some idea of the contribution he made to the war effort. 'There is no doubt that the public has never understood what the Chiefs of Staff have been doing in the running of this war. On the whole the P.M. has never enlightened them much.' So wrote Alanbrooke in his diary towards the end of the war. 'I feel that it is time the country was educated as to how wars are run and strategy controlled.'

I sympathised with Alanbrooke's private comment. When the first volume of his diary was published two years ago I thought there was ample justification for it. Sir Winston had given his own story at great length and it was time that what he had said to those who served him should be supplemented by what they said to him. There was no harm in letting the world know that the great leader in war was a difficult man to manage and that genius had its drawbacks.

All that was accomplished, however, in that first volume. The second one does not add to, and may detract from, Alanbrooke's reputation, and certainly may cast shadows on Anglo-American relations.

In the second volume as in the first we once more see the sapient Chief of the Imperial General Staff struggling to restrain the impulsive action of his master, a master now not infrequently in ill-health, ill-health which he often refuses to have treated, often pretends not to be suffering. 'Don't get in league with that bloody old man,' shouts Winston to Alanbrooke from his sick-bed when the latter echoes some of Lord Moran's warnings.

Pictures of Churchill

The pictures of Winston are splendid. They have all the clarity and swiftness one might expect of a man whose craft was generalship and hobby bird-watching. Winston storming from his bed – 'I do not want any of your long-term policies, they only cripple initiative'; Winston in his vast Mexican sun hat eating soup with one hand and swatting flies with the other – ' "As I was saying, it is all quite simple, there are just three areas. ..." Crash, down came the fly-whisk ...'; Winston the hypochondriac – walking around the interior of his aeroplane with a thermometer in his hand; Winston the intriguer sending off cables to Roosevelt behind Alanbrooke's back, and not even telling the secretaries what he is doing.

There is a classic description of Winston's behaviour at the crossing of the Rhine when, having bullied his way much farther forward into the presence of the enemy than he should have been allowed to, the generals pulled themselves together and ordered him back:–

> ... the U.S. General Simpson, on whose front we were, coming up to Winston and saying: 'Prime Minister, there are snipers in front of you; they are shelling both sides of the bridge and now they have started shelling the road behind you. I cannot accept the responsibility for your being here and must ask you to come away.' The look on Winston's face was just like that of a small boy being called away from his sand-castles on the beach by his nurse! He put both his arms round one of the twisted girders of the bridge and looked over his shoulder at Simpson with pouting mouth and angry eyes.
>
> I can just see that look.

The kind of trouble Alanbrooke had with Churchill will be familiar to readers of the first volume, and the most important aspect of this book is the light it adds – the fuel some will say – to the differences that arose between the Allies as to what was the correct global strategy.

It is very important, I think, in reading this book to understand that not only was there a difference between the views of Alanbrooke and the Americans – with the Russians, of course, continually pressing a third interest – but that there was a difference between those two views and that of Winston.

The whole strategic triangle as it existed when this volume opens, in the autumn of 1943, is described in passages on pages forty-three and seventy-one. Alanbrooke wanted everything that could be spared from the building up of the cross-Channel invasion force to be used in Italy, so as to keep the enemy on tenterhooks all along the South coast of France, Italy and the Aegean, so that they would be unable to reinforce either the forces opposite our cross-Channel build-up or those holding the Russians on the Eastern front. The Americans, however, were continually pressing for a campaign in Burma with a view to reopening the land supply route to Chiang Kai-shek in China.

Basic Difference of Attitude

Winston wanted something else. He had seen that as the Americans put more and more men, money and machines into action they would come to exercise more influence over the conduct of the war. Britain might become a junior partner. He sought to re-establish Britain's power to call the shots by finding some theatre of war where Britain could excel on her own.

Thus, he propounded such schemes as the invasion of Sumatra by Mountbatten which, in the context of Alanbrooke's non-political strategic thinking, were irresponsible, indeed 'absurd.' If this basic difference between Winston's and Alanbrooke's attitudes is not appreciated, much of Winston's role as described in this book seems both reprehensible and incomprehensible. Having paid deference occasionally to Winston's political attitude to strategic possibilities, Alanbrooke himself is inclined to write for the most part as though he had forgotten them, and as though Winston could have been expected to take as limited a military view of the war effort as he was able to do himself.

The initial strategic differences between us and the Americans must be understood because out of them developed the issues which became controversial. The Americans were persuaded to divert resources from the Far East and put them into the campaign in North Africa with the greatest reluctance. There was need for great diplomacy on the part of the commanders in the field in North Africa, therefore, and it was because he excelled at promoting unity between potential quarrellers that the comparatively unknown and inexperienced American General Dwight Eisenhower came to the fore. Eisenhower's gifts displayed here became increasingly important as the war went on, and undoubtedly they performed the greatest service in the Allied cause.

When it was clear that the direction of the Channel invasion must also go to an American, partly because of the sheer numbers of American troops involved, partly to counter Admiral King's attempt to make the Japanese not the Germans the main objective, General Eisenhower was given supreme command of

Overlord. Here again in all the preparations for this great adventure General Eisenhower's particular qualities found ample scope.

View Still the Same

By the eve of D-Day, however, Alanbrooke had made up his mind that General Eisenhower was a soldier of limited ability. In his diary for May 15, 1944, he records:—

> *The main impression I gathered [at Eisenhower's final run-over plans for the invasion] was that Eisenhower was no real director of thought, plans, energy or direction. Just a co-ordinator, a good mixer, a champion of inter-Allied co-operation, and in those respects few can hold the candle to him. But is that enough? Or can we not find all qualities of a commander in one man? May be I am getting too hard to please, but I doubt it.*

Commenting after the war was over on what he said in his diary at the time, Alanbrooke says:—

> *If I was asked to review the opinion I expressed that evening of Eisenhower, I should, in the light of all later experience, repeat every word of it. A past-master in the handling of allies, entirely impartial and consequently trusted by all. A charming personality and good co-ordinator. But no real commander ... Ike might have been a showman calling on various actors to perform their various turns, but he was not the commander of the show who controlled and directed all the actors. A very different performance from Monty's show a few days previously.*

If this was Alanbrooke's attitude to Eisenhower at a time when Eisenhower's gifts were paying dividends, it can be anticipated that when the European war entered a phase in which Eisenhower's limitations became evident, Alanbrooke would be even more critical. And this was to be the case.

Effect on U.S. Relations

Eisenhower took the courageous decision to go ahead with the invasion despite the danger of unfavourable weather, and under his generalship the landings were successfully effected. Once the bridgehead had been secured, however, there was the need of a broad strategic plan and a mind that would carry it out with vigour and clear purpose. As is generally known, a controversy developed between those who believed with Eisenhower that once a breakthrough had been effected there should be an attack the whole length of the line with Bradley's, Patton's and Montgomery's armies engaged; and those, like Montgomery, who wanted a concentrated attack on the Ruhr to deal a knockout blow at a reeling enemy.

Since this argument has already been thrashed out – as it was once said – to everybody's dissatisfaction, it is a pity that it has to be thrashed out once more in a way which yields nothing novel except some observations about the capacities of the present President of the United States which are not likely to improve Anglo-American relations.

That Eisenhower did not do what Montgomery and Alanbrooke wanted is attributed in the diary to the fact that he was 'essentially a staff officer with little knowledge of the realities of the battlefield ... obsessed with logistical problems ... a very, very limited brain from a strategic point of view. ... He only sees the worse side of Monty and cannot appreciate the better side. ...' (The last not a great indictment of Ike, I should have thought.)

Alanbrooke, of course, was deeply worried. We had pretty well scraped the barrel to launch the invasion in full force, and now the war looked like going on much longer than we had reckoned for.

'Unauthorised Wire to Stalin'

'Eisenhower's new plan to take command in Northern France on September 1,' he noted, 'is likely to add another three to six months on to the war.' Later, 'Eisenhower, though supposed to be doing so [i.e., running one co-ordinated land battle instead of letting Monty, Patton and Bradley run three battles], is on the golf links at Rheims and taking practically no part in the running of the war.'

The indictment culminates in the charge that instead of letting Monty, when his bridgehead on the other side of the Rhine was thirty-five miles long and twenty-five deep, with twenty divisions and 1,500 tanks across, sweep forward across the Hanover plains to the Elbe and Berlin, Eisenhower dispatched an unauthorised telegram to Stalin. In this Eisenhower informed Stalin that he proposed after encircling the Ruhr to concentrate on central Germany, then make for the upper Elbe, there to await the arrival of the Russians, his object being to cut Germany in half and concentrate his main forces against the supposed 'national redoubt' in the Austrian Alps, in which, it was rumoured, Hitler and his Nazi fanatics intended to make a last stand. Had Eisenhower gone straight for Berlin, of course, we would have got there before the Russians, and history might have been very different.

The facts are as Alanbrooke gives them, and in my view Monty was right and Ike was wrong. But Alanbrooke goes too far, much too far, in imputing blame to Eisenhower personally.

Philosophy, Not Personalities

What is really wrong about one soldier blaming another is that the political considerations which govern the military leave the generals far less free than they think they are. And human nature being what it is they are prone to get fed up with the generals on the other side of the alliance in about the same degree as with the politicians on *their* side. President Eisenhower is a national hero in the United States and the very forceful comments on his capacity as a general which appear in this volume are likely to be unpalatable.

To my mind the volume should have been held over until the prominent actors have passed from the stage. And in any case we can do without personal comments. Differences as to major strategy may well be a subject of argument on a high philosophical level, but estimates of personal capacity, especially when formed in the peculiar circumstances in which a private diary is written, tend to rouse heat.

And the personalities are of limited importance. Eisenhower's refusal to push on to Berlin, though partly the result of imperfect strategy, was really attributable to American delusions about Russia which Eisenhower, though he shared them, did not create. The Americans were indeed innocents abroad. It is ironical to reflect when one considers their present attitude to the Communist peril, how much they contributed to its extension westward.

Putting Comment in Context

Put in context, these references to Eisenhower need not do much damage. Take, for instance, a major question – his capacity as a military commander. In a letter from Alanbrooke to Montgomery there is a passage which is bound to be given wide publicity in the United States. 'You have told me,' says Alanbrooke, 'and I have agreed with you, that Ike was no commander, that he has no strategic vision, was incapable of making a plan or of running operations when started.'

This sounds pretty categoric. However, it should be remembered that when he wrote this letter, Alanbrooke was doing his best to restrain Montgomery from getting across Eisenhower, and was very wisely attempting to humour Monty in order the better to control him.

Moreover, there is enough criticism of Monty in this book to support the view that the Americans could be forgiven for ignoring Monty's advice, even when it was, in fact, well founded. Indeed, in spite of Alanbrooke's praise of Monty, there is such testimony to his mischievousness that it is a toss-up which of the two, Ike or Monty, seems to have given our C.I.G.S. the greater headache.

Monty was always convinced of the rightness of his own views, in which he was not infrequently correct. But he had no tact. When, on one occasion, Bradley came round to Monty's way of thinking, Alanbrooke wrote to Monty and begged him, when he next encountered Bradley, not to rub this in. Monty, characteristically, rubbed it in good and proper.

Command Set-up Faulty

I do not myself think that any competent soldier would disagree with the judgment that the set-up of the command in France was faulty and that Eisenhower's attempt to be at the same time supreme commander and commander of the land forces was a mistake. Indeed, it seems that Bedell Smith, a very able American general, made representations to him that he was not really running the war. Eisenhower seemed embedded in the theory of attack all along the line, the theory being reinforced by the curious doctrine that every general must have an equal and fair share of the battle. Alanbrooke has the right to feel this was wrong, but in publishing his diary it is a pity that, before including passages like those I have quoted, he had not recalled that the best possible relations between the two great leading democratic countries are as vital now as ever.

I have more confidence in the inherent health and resilience of those relations than to feel they will be much damaged by this book. Alanbrooke, of course, has his lapses of judgment. Several times – and as early as 1944 – he suggests that Winston had, so to speak, 'had it,' was 'finished,' whereas sixteen years later that human battleship is still afloat. Alanbrooke's unreserved praise for MacArthur, and particularly his view that he was a great man whereas Marshall was second-rate, will not be accepted by many Americans, while his strictures on Winston's imaginative and prescient views on the effect of the discovery of the atomic bomb, delivered the day they heard about Hiroshima, are so wide of the mark that they must be written off as those of a particularly tired brain.

To say that Alanbrooke's Diary is anti-American is positively misleading. Quantitatively it is considerably more anti-British, with accounts of British generals threatening to resign, of the British Chiefs of Staff considering resigning in a body, and of Alanbrooke himself considering resigning as a protest against the treatment meted out to them by the wicked Winston. As has been said, there is only one thing worse than the difficulty of carrying on war in company with allies – that is to have no allies. A war leader who comes out of the book well is Stalin, who is not often mentioned, but whose judgment in military matters Alanbrooke admired.

The result of the 1945 election disappointed Alanbrooke deeply, though in view of what he said previously about Winston in his diary one might be forgiven for thinking any change would have been agreeable to him. But Alanbrooke missed him. Although he had been at times driven almost to distraction by his vagaries, he lost the stimulus of constant contact with that colourful personality. Moreover, he had struck up a remarkable working partnership with the Secretary of State for War, Mr. P. J. Grigg.

The change did him good, however. He now had to deal with an ordinary man in No. 10, and he came to admire Grigg's successor, Lord Lawson.

Good Terms with Bevin

Much as he deplored what he thought of as a change of horses when the stream of war still flowed, with characteristic fair-mindedness he recognised that the change of Government in the post-war period was desirable. He recognised the inevitability of freedom for India. He was soon on good terms with Ernest Bevin. My relations with him led me to like and respect a fine character and a brilliant mind.

Indeed the only thing for which I would criticise Alanbrooke is the publication of this second volume. And this raises the whole question again of whether – memoirs apart – diaries like these should be published.

I have said in connection with Montgomery's memoirs that it is largely a matter of timing. It is essential that secrets, especially the secrets of the mistakes – you soon get to know about the triumphs – should be made known as soon as possible. Thereby a democracy obtains the confidence of access to the facts and the practical lessons which may be drawn from them. But 'as soon as possible' is a matter for judgment.

There is, too, the question of what value should be set upon a private diary, and on one supplemented as this one is by a commentary upon the jottings that is written long after the events. The diary in its pure form by its nature represents a point of view limited by time, place and emotion, if not by knowledge. It tends to bind the writer so that his commentary must follow, emphasise, what he has already written, take that as the main starting point, not the truer picture which may have emerged. If, on the other hand, the writer is to free himself from these bonds, this frequently means denying the value of what he wrote. If a diary is to enable tense minds to let off steam in private, it cannot be regarded as a safe historical source; and if it is written for use as a future historical document, it is suspect for the opposite reason. One cannot have it both ways.

18

What Sort of Man Gets to the Top?

At all times and in all political societies there will be no shortage
of people ready, and indeed eager, to participate actively in
political life, though whether the supply of men of the right
quality is adequate is a very different matter.

The questions arise, therefore: 'Why do people go into
politics?' and 'What are the qualities needed in a democratic,
parliamentary leader?'

I think that a society which can give a satisfactory answer to
these questions is not only more likely to have a good supply of
people ready to undertake the hazards of a political career, but is
also more likely to have plenty of first-class men in public life.

An Ambition to be Premier

Most men who go into politics and become Members of the
House of Commons would like to be Prime Minister.

I say 'most men,' not by any means 'all men.' You always find
a number of men in the House of Commons who have gone in
there not because political life in itself attracts them, but because
they have wanted to get something done and have gone into the
House of Commons because they have thought that that was the
best way to get it done. Among these men you will find
missionaries on the one hand, and men who are virtually the
representatives of special interests on the other.

You will also find a number of men who are genuinely too
modest, too indolent, or too little interested in competition for
power – or too absorbed in the intellectual side of politics – to
wish to be anything but backbenchers. Such men occasionally

find some greatness thrust upon them, usually when power is evenly divided among three or four strenuous contenders, and some kind of compromise choice is needed.

But, as I say, on the whole most men who go into the House of Commons would like to become Prime Minister.

How is it done?

I suppose a great many people get it into their heads at school that the most important thing to be able to do in the House of Commons is to make good speeches. It depends what you mean by 'good speeches.' One of the most memorable speeches made in the House of Commons in my time was the famous speech made by Amery in 1940. Speaking from the same side of the House as Neville Chamberlain, the Leader of the Conservative Party, Amery criticised his handling of the war, and, ending his speech in the famous words of Cromwell, cried: 'You have sat too long here for any good you have been doing. ... In the name of God, go.'

India Speech by Lord Halifax

This speech marked the end of Chamberlain's dominion within the Conservative Party, and almost immediately afterwards the Conservative Administration came to an end and a Coalition Government was formed with Mr. Churchill (as he then was) at its head and myself as Deputy Prime Minister.

Amery was no orator. He was a man of great ability but not exciting to listen to. His 'great' speech did not 'do' anything; its 'greatness' was that it 'marked' something. The fact that Amery said what he did may have influenced a few people, but it was the fact that he had said the things he did about his leader, not how he said them, that mattered.

One of the most influential speeches made in my time was made in the House of Lords by Lord Halifax, on the granting of independence to India in 1948. The Lords were going to divide on the issue – there was a great deal of resistance to my Government's Bill. After Halifax had spoken, however, they decided not to.

Halifax, again, was a man of tremendous ability, and character. This was what 'spoke' in the Lords, not his oratory. Halifax was no orator: on the contrary, he was rather dry to listen to. But the Lords knew that Halifax knew India, and they knew that he would tell them the truth. It was his knowledge and his character that swayed them, not his oratory.

The fact that a man of Halifax's calibre is 'for' or 'against' something really matters much more than anything he will say about the subject. Such men do not need powers of persuasion among those who know them.

It is much the same with Lord Salisbury. In my view, Salisbury has been the strongest character in the post-war Conservative Party. Certainly the ablest. He had a great deal of influence in post-war Conservative Cabinets. All the more remarkable in that he was a Peer, and in some ways personally not very sympathetic to many Conservative leaders.

Again, Salisbury had great personal knowledge, was an extremely able man, and spoke the truth. And, of course, he was a Cecil. The Cecils don't give a damn. That makes a lot of difference.

This doesn't mean that there are no occasions in the House of Commons – or at party conferences – when the ability to sway an audience by argument rather than character is very important. Ernest Bevin was not much of an orator. As a speaker he was rough and ready. But when Ernest was set on something, and believed in it, he could and did sway votes by persuasion – he could be irresistible, as when repudiating George Lansbury's pacifist speech at the Labour Party conference at Brighton in 1935.

Keynes's Feat of Persuasion

Another great feat of persuasion was that of Keynes in the Lords at the time when a great many of them wished to refuse the American loan. Keynes made a lucid and persuasive speech, which shut them up.

What counts most in the House of Commons is being respected. On both sides. As a man.

I have often been asked what it is that makes a Member respected. I would say it is very simple: a man has to know his stuff; he mustn't talk too much; he must be good-tempered; not conceited; and be known to be a decent chap.

One of the most influential men in my time was Lord Addison. The Labour Party owed a great deal to him. A wonderful man in the House of Commons and in the House of Lords. No orator. No art.

Patience, friendliness, common sense – these were his virtues – nobody wanted to quarrel when Addison was around. He made it seem wrong.

Mistake of the Small-Minded

Judging by some of the views I have seen expressed about politicians in the last few years, it is quite likely that one of these days somebody will be saying that Addison was a Machiavellian manipulator of men. There is always a tendency for men with small minds, and a great deal of selfishness in their natures, to assume that if one man succeeds in getting others to work with him, he is endowed with an even greater fund of self-seeking qualities than they are aware of having themselves.

There are many men who find it impossible to believe that men lead others by such things as the example of moral or physical courage; sympathy; self-discipline; altruism; and superior capacity for hard work. They also seem to feel that any clash between two leaders is due either to a passionate struggle, or to self-seeking ambition on the part of one or the other. In fact, however, a lieutenant may often challenge his leader because he genuinely feels that he should.

I personally was very fortunate in that I did not experience the testing times that other leaders of parties have done. At all times it was clear to me that certain jobs had to be done, and I had to make up my mind, with the assistance of my colleagues, about who was the best man to do them.

Sometimes I had to remove men from office. When I had made up my mind, I tried to act on it as quickly as possible and without beating about the bush. I paid my colleagues the compliment which above all I would like to have had paid me: I assumed that we were all doing what we were out of a real sense of mission, and that at any moment, if it was clear to the majority of us that somebody had to go, he would accept it in exactly the same spirit of service in which he had taken the post in the first place.

I was never conscious of any intrigue against me. I would have taken no notice of rumours, suggestions or hints. When I heard in 1935 that they were talking about my becoming the leader of the party, I did not know whether I was going to be proposed, let alone know who was going to propose me. I would have thought it unbecoming, improper, and ultimately ineffective, to try to find out, even if I had not been too shy to do so.

Only Authority Worth Having

Just as a man cannot be a leader for long if he is not trusted, he cannot be a leader for long if he cannot trust. The only kind of authority worth having is what is given without being sought for.

Men who lobby their way forward into leadership are the most likely to be lobbied back out of it. The man who has most control of his followers is the man who shows no fear. And a man cannot be a leader if he is afraid of losing his job.

There is a great deal of influence, of course, to be exerted in the Labour Party *outside* the House of Commons. Again, much the same qualities are required and again speech-making is of only limited importance.

Indeed, people who talk too much soon find themselves up against it. Harold Laski, for instance. A brilliant chap, but he talked too much. A wonderful teacher – you must be able to talk to teach, and we need all the teachers we can get – but no political judgment.

Another Brilliant Chap

He wanted to be a public figure and an *eminence grise* at the same time. You can't be both. I gave him a try as an *eminence grise*, but he started making speeches at the week-ends. I had to get rid of him.

And, of course, the leader or potential leader must be in touch, if only intuitively, with the rank and file. G. D. H. Cole was another brilliant chap. A very clear mind. But he used to have a new idea every year, irrespective of whether the ordinary man was interested in it or not.

The question of keeping in touch with the rank and file is highly important. It is highly important from the point of view of the working of the democratic machine, but it is also very important to the man who wants to be an effective leader. Stanley Baldwin did not seem to like talking with his own rank and file, though he enjoyed long talks on the terrace with Labour Members, especially miners. But he always seemed to know what was going on, at any rate in his prime.

19
Flaws at the Top

On the whole, I think our leaders are less in touch with the man in the street than they were fifty years ago.

It has to do partly with the question of what takes chaps into politics now as opposed to what took them into politics then. Fifty years ago, most Labour Members fetched up in the House of Commons because they had got disturbed about what they saw around them in the places they lived in or knew, and felt the way to get something done about them was to get into the House.

Keeping in touch with the ordinary man was not a problem. It was because they were in touch with the ordinary bloke that they thought about going into the House in the first place.

Nowadays, there are quite a lot of chaps who are in the House because the idea of sitting in Westminster and helping to govern the country appeals to them. They keep in touch with feeling in the constituencies, of course; they go back to them; hold their 'surgeries' at week-ends. But somehow it's different.

Another thing is that life is more complicated and government more complex. An M.P. has to read a great deal – reports, economic surveys, and Bills. The Welfare State has required additional laws and regulations.

The men of my generation had to go through the mill. When I became a Socialist it meant that most members of the middle class, to which I belonged, felt that I had done something despicable.

Real Persecution

Most members of the middle class who became Socialists had a pretty miserable time. You had to feel pretty strongly about your convictions to get through: you had to be willing to go out and be shot at.

A young Socialist lawyer would find that Liberal or Tory lawyers would not be willing to give him briefs. The parents of the girl he wanted to marry, and who wanted to marry him, would look down their noses at him. In some cases there would be real social persecution.

Today it is perfectly all right socially – and morally – to be middle class (even upper class) and believe in Socialism. Moreover, if you want to do something useful and constructive about social problems you can do it without becoming any less respectable. There are plenty of organisations which you can join, even if you are an Old Etonian, without people thinking you 'red.' They might think you stupid, but not dangerous.

It was good for the men of my generation to be for many years a small minority. And it was good for us, in a different way, later, to be members of a small minority in Parliament. It was hard at the time, of course.

It was especially good for us to go back to being a tiny minority in the thirties after having been a majority in the twenties. It gave us a sense of pace and a sense of proportion – very valuable things for a leader to have.

In the thirties, with just forty-five of us there you had to be able to get up and speak on anything. With that great mass of Tories opposite you, you learned to grin and bear it. And, of course, you learned a great deal sitting there day after day, night after night.

Just Watching

I think the young men – and the older men – who came into Parliament as part of a huge Labour majority didn't get the training we got. It's a good thing for leaders of the House of Commons to have sat for some time in Opposition. Not too long. Too long a period of Opposition stales the mind. That was the trouble with the German Social Democrats: they had to criticise for so long they lost the faculty for being constructive.

If you could plan these things, I think it would be a good thing for everybody to start in the House of Commons in Opposition. I think the Labour M.P. who starts off on the Government side misses something, and the man who starts off virtually as a Labour Minister, as several did just after the war, misses much more.

It's useful to have to sit in Opposition for your first few years, but it is particularly good for people to have to sit there unable to say very much while the ex-Ministers and the Privy Councillors are being called on all the time. Young chaps like me had to just sit there and keep quiet; but we could listen and watch points. Very important. Whoever the man is, and whatever his gifts of leadership, he needs a great deal of experience of the House of Commons.

If he doesn't obtain the respect of his own party (and of the other side; I have yet to learn of a case in which a man who did not enjoy a great deal of respect from the Opposition had the respect of his own party) he will not get far in politics. He certainly will not get to the top.

In my lifetime the classic example of this is Lord Beaverbrook. People below the age of fifty, I am sure, do not realise how much this man counted in British politics during the First World War. He was worth millions of pounds, he had a great influence upon the Press – at a time when the influence of the Press was not only at its peak but was credited with being even higher. And he had, there is no doubt about it, a number of highly developed personal gifts – including a bold and colourful character – of the greatest political usefulness. But he did not obtain real political power, nor has he since. Not enough of his own party – let alone chaps on the other side of the House – trusted him.

Lord Northcliffe was another, and similar example.

A leader has got to be trusted. When men start distrusting him he stops being a leader.

Mention of Lord Beaverbrook reminds me that next to character – or integrity – comes judgment. I put them in that order because true judgment is found, in my view, only in men of character. Judgment, indeed, presupposes character. Judgment comes from the capacity of learning from one's mistakes, which requires humility.

Nervous Strain

A man may rise to the top without judgment, but he will not stay there very long. Sir Anthony Eden is the best example of this I know.

Judgment, at any rate when exercised over a long period in everyday practical politics, is rarely found in men who do not have a strong physical constitution. Only men of very strong constitution can stand up to the nervous and physical strain of prolonged argument, especially in time of crisis.

An equable temperament, a strong constitution, and freedom from any excessive appetite of any kind are the three most important bases of a good, sound judgment. A man who lacks one of them will not be in a position of political power long before coming a cropper, and bringing his party down into the bargain.

Judgment is required in order to be able to deal with men and with matters of moment. The problem of getting a Cabinet to work together is a profoundly difficult one, one which is to a very great extent veiled by the tradition of Cabinet secrecy and Cabinet responsibility.

A good leader must understand human nature, and particularly the human nature of the particular group of men he has as his lieutenants, in relation to the particular stresses and strains of the day. He must also have good tactical judgment – know what issues to exploit in the House of Commons, how to make the most of them, and which ones to go easy on. You can't conduct a full-out dialectical battle on the floor of the House of Commons from the beginning of a Parliamentary session to the end, with everything full out the whole time.

There are the weak points and the strong points in the enemy's case. A good Leader of the Opposition must be capable of leaping to his feet within a moment or two of the announcement of a new move by the Government, and attacking it in terms which the whole of his party can immediately grasp and rise to.

Ready to Act

On the other hand, he must be equally capable of holding himself on a tight rein, and making sure that in the interests of getting off to a flying start he will not compromise the Opposition's case. In cricketing language, he has to be ready and willing to go out and hook one off his eyebrows over the pavilion: but he has also got to move over and let a fast one go by the off-stump without nibbling at it, whatever the barrackers say.

Courage is important. A leader must have it in order to make big decisions which may, even if they are the correct ones, make him look a fool, a coward, or a renegade, in the short, or even the long, term. Decisions about sacking people are often harder than those about policy. If he doesn't display courage, the chances are that he will never become the leader, or that if he does, he won't last very long.

A leader must have guts. He must be ready to act swiftly however much he has sweated about what is the right thing to do. Grown men, who know the score, do not want their leader to be continually beating his breast, and advertising his agonies. They want decision and action. Self-examination in public is the privilege of the rank and file.

Finally, of course, a man who wishes to lead in politics must, on balance, enjoy being a politician. By enjoying, I don't mean the excitement and the pleasure of it, but the much deeper satisfaction that comes to a man who believes that what he is doing does honour to himself and his friends and is of social value.

We hear a great deal, nowadays, about the alleged intrigue, knifing and back-biting in politics. I think it is worth while bearing in mind that this kind of picture of politics is created largely by the politicians who have failed to get to the top. The kind of politician who leaks to the Press, or gossips to the third-rate novelist, is, in my experience, usually just that intriguing, egoistically ambitious and feuding kind of personality who fails to be accepted as a leader.

There is one thing about politics that I think cannot be disputed: if a man stays in them long enough, they nearly always reveal him for what he is, and he tends to get not only what he deserves, but to find in his fate the reflection of his own strength and weakness.

The intriguers are usually the victims of intrigue. The indiscreet usually perish by their indiscretion. Politicians sometimes get stabbed in the back; more usually it is the fault in their heel that destroys them.

20

A Name for Loyalty

Somebody said recently that the two most important political figures in Britain between the two world wars were Ernest Bevin and Stanley Baldwin. Certainly, both men exerted tremendous influence upon their parties, mainly by defeating or containing the extremists; Baldwin by subtle diplomacy, Bevin by open war.

Neither planned or carried out concrete formative policies. They were stabilisers, rather than propellers, very necessary when big ships are rolling in heavy seas.

With Baldwin I shall deal on another occasion. A few reflections on Ernie Bevin are stimulated by the appearance of the first volume of his definitive biography by Alan Bullock.*

This is a massive work about a massive man. I think it is quite brilliant. Bullock has set out to tell fully the story of Ernest Bevin and his times at a length worthy of its subject. In this first volume he gives us the life story of a great man up to his fifty-ninth year. Had he died then he would have had behind him the record of the greatest leader in the history of the trade union movement. But in the next eleven years he was to become a great statesman, the man who organised the men and women of Britain behind the fighting forces in the greatest crisis in her history and the man who was acknowledged to be a great Foreign Secretary.

A Place in History

In other lives the years before a man steps into the limelight as a statesman might be considered merely formative, but here,

The Life and Times of Ernest Bevin. Vol. I. Trade Union Leader, 1881–1940. Heinemann, 1960.

although preceding experience gave abundant results when the time came, Bevin's achievement as set out in this first volume entitles him to a place in history. When I first knew the trade union movement its characteristic was its disunity. There were numbers of small unions organised locally on a craft basis. It expressed the partialism and conservatism of the British working man. Though its slogan was Unity is Strength, its practice was disunity and weakness. Since those days there have been amalgamations and the growth of powerful unions with wealth running into hundreds of thousands, but no one would have expected that the greatest impetus to unity would have come from one of the weakest, poorest and most disunited industries, transport. That it did so was mainly due to Ernest Bevin, a Bristol carman who did not begin his career until he was thirty.

Mr. Bullock is particularly good in recalling the background of Bevin's labours. It is difficult for the younger generation to recall that in those days the railway directors refused to meet the representatives of their workers, then organised under the humble name of The Amalgamated Society of Railway Servants. Victimisation of trade unionists was still common and generally trade unionism was still regarded by the better-fed classes as a conspiracy. Mr. Bullock has had access to exceptional documentation and has used it well. His story is vividly told and brought back to me very graphically the atmosphere of the period.

Ernie was a very big man with a wide range of qualities. But what stands out in my view of him was his loyalty. Loyalty is a great virtue in private life, and an even greater one in the stormy seas of politics – second only to courage, with which indeed it goes hand in hand. Ernest was the living symbol of loyalty, and its most consistent exponent. He was especially loyal to working people both at home and abroad. Though no violent proponent of the class-war, he was profoundly conscious in everything he did, whether in home or foreign affairs, of the working people and their interests. There was class consciousness in his nature: no class hatred. People are inclined to get the two confused.

Break-up of Family

I have heard it said that a man must have a sense of security to be loyal. If this is so, Ernest's loyalty is all the more remarkable. He took his name from his mother's husband, but she had left William Bevin years before Ernest was born and the identity of his real father is unknown. His mother died when he was eight and the night she was buried the family was broken up deliberately and methodically, each child going off to live with a relative or a friend, never to meet as a family again.

Ernest was passionately attached to his mother, a remarkable woman, a resolute Methodist and temperance worker, when to be these things in a country village was to affront the moral and social authority of the hard-drinking local Tory farmer. In view of the way fate ripped him from her, it is hard to see where Ernie's sense of security came from.

For Ernest loyalty was a practical as well as a moral virtue. The huge federation he built up out of thirty-seven smaller unions would not have lasted long if loyalty had not been its cardinal virtue. Disloyalty was the ultimate political crime. Curiously enough, his loyalty went with a personality in which the capacity for being suspicious was remarkably developed.

Walking with a Roll

Another paradox had to do with his self-confidence. Ernest, walking slowly through a conference hall to board the platform, rolling slightly from side to side like a battleship, seemed the embodiment of self-confidence. He would square-up to anybody, physically or morally, with relish – Churchill, for instance, at the height of his prestige in the Second World War. Ernie treated him as an equal. But within his union he surrounded himself with lieutenants whom he knew he could dominate. He was sensitive to criticism. He never cared for number twos who could argue with him.

But once he gave you his trust he was like a rock. In 1948 one or two members of my Government suggested that I should resign in favour of someone else. I would have paid no attention to intrigue, even if I had known about it, but if it was clear that I had lost the general support of the party, of course, I would have gone. I thought it right to go to somebody I trusted, say I was ready to go if it were in the public interest and ask for an objective view. 'If you go, I go with you, Clem,' said Bevin. 'You ought to stay.' That was enough for me. If Ernie thought I should go, he would have said so.

If he was behind me nobody was capable of causing trouble. Only Ernie had any real prospect of succeeding me.

With the capacity for being loyal went a capacity for inspiring loyalty. Particularly on his way up to the top, Ernest made a lot of enemies, but on the whole, he was a much loved man. It wasn't so remarkable that he was admired and respected when he was at the Ministry of Labour. (His Conservative Under-Secretaries were devoted to him.) More remarkable was the affection he inspired at the Foreign Office. Everybody spoke well of him, from the Ambassadors to the cleaners. He inspired loyalty because he understood people and showed it. He treated people as human beings, regardless of rank. He inquired into the conditions and pay of the women who cleaned the floor and he altered the regulations so that the passages of wives of Ambassadors coming home on holiday were paid for at the same rate as their husbands'.

Ernest looked, and indeed *was*, the embodiment of common sense. Yet I have never met a man in politics with as much imagination as he had, with the exception of Winston. On the personal level it manifested itself in telling anecdotes in which he painted character and situation in vivid colours. He would hold forth at great length in the Cabinet, in the most egotistical artistic way, much the same way as Winston would.

Even when he was a young agitator, he was an impresario as well. In Bristol, at the age of twenty-seven, a member of the local branch of the Social Democratic Federation, Ernest was called upon to organise 'Right-to-Work' demonstrations. In other places these were untidy, rough and aggressive operations. In Bristol it was different.

One Sunday morning, the congregation of the cathedral, standing at the beginning of the service, found a long column of unemployed filing quietly into the nave, taking up their position in the aisles. After the service, the men formed up again outside the cathedral and, led by Bevin, marched off and dispersed. The silent, orderly demonstration had a most dramatic effect.

Dockers' K.C. Title

It was as a result of the good effects of this demonstration that Ernest became a trade unionist: later, during a strike of port workers, he was asked to organise the local carters and make them a branch of the Dockers' Union, since carters in those days worked chiefly in and around the port along with the dockers. Bevin himself was driving a mineral water dray at the time.

Later, his sense of the dramatic gave him success on a wider platform. He pleaded the case of the dockers in 1920 in a most dramatic manner. On one occasion, he put ten plates before the members of the Court. They contained the tiny portion of cabbage, potatoes and meat which the employers considered adequate to sustain the strength of a docker hauling seventy-one tons of wheat a day on his shoulders. This was when he became known as 'the Dockers' K.C.'

He had that great gift, *practical* imagination. He was able to do things which made you appreciate imagination, working on the most mundane level, but he had intellectual vision too. The creation of the Transport and General Workers' Union on a *double* basis of representation by trades and also by geographical area, though it sounds simple enough, was a brilliant idea. His imagination ranged abroad. At the Edinburgh T.U.C. in 1927, he was saying that 'the spirit of a United States of Europe – at least on an economic basis ...' was the only solution to Europe's problem, and was proposing a European customs union. Twelve years later he startled the Southport Conference of the Labour Party by proposing an economic union between the Western democracies and the Commonwealth.

His imagination took him over the barriers his prejudices might have put up for him. When he went to the United States and Canada on an industry and trade union delegation, led by the Minister of Labour in 1927, he noted the growing divorce between ownership and management in the United States and pondered its implications. 'I frankly confess in my job, the large-scale organisation of labour, I feel more akin with this type [the manager of large-scale business organisation] than I do with so-called directors.'

As a negotiator, Bevin was superb. Lord Citrine, who should be an excellent judge, says that he had 'never met Bevin's equal, had certainly never met his superior, in negotiation.' He was patient, and his tremendous stamina – so essential to negotiation – stood him in good stead. His sense of drama enabled him to break off negotiations with tremendous flourish, if he thought it would serve his case. He had the quickness of mind and the power of swift association which enables the negotiator to make capital out of anything and everything.

There was an interesting case when he was negotiating with the London Passenger Board. He staggered Lord Ashfield by coming back into the conference room and saying, 'We'll consolidate at six shillings, and wash out the cost of living, shall we?' The Passenger Board were pleased to settle – the cost of living increment had worried them. It turned out later that during the lunch-time break, Ernie had bumped into an official of the Ministry of Labour. In a chat about things in general, the official mentioned that it was expected now that the cost of living would go down.

Knowledge of U.S. Labour

He had a remarkable memory and a great facility for assimilating information and keeping it handy. He knew a great deal about American labour, even before the First World War and visited America in 1915. He went on delegations to international trade union meetings in Europe in the twenties and thirties. In 1923, when he was concerned about what the French were doing in the Ruhr, the Transport and General Workers' Union sent their own committee to find out what was going on. Years before he went to the Foreign Office, he had a vast knowledge of industrial, financial and social conditions in many different countries.

There was the occasion of the Belgian lock-out. The Belgian workers came over to see Ernest when he was still secretary of the Transport and General Workers' Union, and said if they couldn't get some financial help, the lock-out would succeed. 'I'll let you have £100,000,' said Ernest. He knew, if anything better than they did, what they were up against. Because of a mistake made by an assistant the cheque was drawn for a million. Within a few hours of the cheque's being drawn, the Belgian bank had got in touch with the Belgian employers and had said to them virtually: 'Those chaps have just got a million pounds put into the kitty. You might as well give up.' The lock-out came to a speedy end.

I have heard it said that his memory was much developed by having to go home every Sunday night from chapel at the ages of five and six, and tell his mother what the preacher had said in the sermon. He certainly exercised it by a habit of not reading books. Life and the men he met were Ernest's books and he drew on them freely. This, with his exuberant and unselfconscious egotism, frequently involved him in plagiarism.

One of the expressions of his unselfconscious egotism, perhaps, was his attitude to the King's English. His grammar was improvised. He never bothered about the difference between the singular and the plural. He seemed not to care. Aitches were of no consequence. There are some people who can be told how to pronounce 'Gandhi' at weekly intervals, but who will still continue to pronounce it 'Gandeye' to the day they die. Ernest was like that. He was quite unabashed. 'Now, you girls, go and put that into English,' he would say to his secretaries at the Foreign Office, after dictating. His treatment of foreign words was cavalier. 'A nice little man, Biddle,' he used to say of Bidault. He always called Ramadier 'Remeedier.'

He was slow to grasp the fact that a Parliamentarian had to go about his business in a different way from the trade unionist. If he were in a tight corner in, say, a wage dispute, he could get to his feet, nod to his colleagues and call the process off, resuming, if he so wished, at a later date of his own choosing. He did not have to fight unless he wanted to.

He didn't understand that in Parliament, on the other hand, where the fight went on day in, day out, we couldn't be continually fighting to the death with the men on the other side of the House. We had to live with them. Ernest didn't easily take to the comradeship and tolerance which is a feature – the most important feature – of the House of Commons. It smacked to him of collusion. He thought we should always be hammering the Tories and treating them like cads.

Yet he had absolutely no illusion about 'the working class' having a monopoly of virtue, or a divine right to preferential treatment. Far from it. He was far more bitter towards some of his fellow trade unionists than I ever knew him to be towards an employer or a Tory.

As I have said, there was no class-hatred in his system. Perhaps it was because he had no personal sense of inferiority. He thought he was as good as anybody else in the country and he saw no reason why everybody else should not have the same high opinion of himself.

21

A Man of Power

Ernest Bevin's great contribution to the Labour Movement was to emphasise the importance of power and, having emphasised it, set about obtaining it. Power, and the sense of its importance, came naturally to him.

Physically, he was a powerful man. He knew the importance of power in the form of health and physical strength when, aged thirteen, he was a van-boy on a dray, working in all weather for twelve hours a day, and when, later, he would travel several hundred miles in a week to recruit trade union members at the quayside and on the street corner. He knew the power of voice, fists and feet.

Recognised as a Born Leader

Because of his own genius for organisation and his confidence in his own strength, he did not fear – he embraced – power. Lord Acton's famous dictum on power probably never occurred to him. And if he agreed that power corrupts, he would have said that it corrupted only the men who were not big enough to use it. And power was given to Ernest. Men recognised in him a natural leader, someone to lean on. He attracted power. At a time when the Labour Movement had all the hopes, aspirations, ideas and saints necessary for Utopia, Ernest helped bring its feet to the ground by insisting that these things without power were useless.

To create power, the first thing in Ernest's view was to eliminate internal conflicts and absorb possibly competitive organisations. This was the idea which led to the creation of the Transport and General Workers' Union out of thirty-seven bits and pieces. This organisation, the mammoth of its time, and now 1,250,000 strong, will probably go down to history owing more to Ernest Bevin than to any other single man.

There was a bad side to Ernest's attitude to power. There was no place for the rebel in Ernest's organisation, not, at any rate, in its formative years or in any other time when it might be in danger. He was a 'majorities' man, and was impatient of minorities. In this respect, of course, he ran counter to one of the most important traditions in the Labour Party.

Ernest's attitude to power was a result of his powerful personality, but it was also the fruit of his realistic thinking. For all his imagination, he was a tremendous realist. And at a time when the idealists were in danger of misleading the Labour Movement, his influence was a great corrective. Power and realism are his legacy to the Labour Movement.

Sceptical About Syndicalism

As a twenty-year-old van driver in Bristol he learned his politics mainly from the dockers, who were regarded very much as the spearhead of the Labour Movement. The dockers' Socialism was of the syndicalist hue. Ernest, however, was always sceptical about syndicalism. The syndicalists wanted to organise power to be able to launch a general strike, which would bring the State to the ground and enable a new order to be set up. This was not what Ernest was organising for. What he wanted was 'not so much ... power to attack [as] power to negotiate.' Like the syndicalists, he was interested in a new order but 'I stand for social revolution brought about by a freely elected Parliament.' (Bristol, 1918.)

Where he was in sympathy with the syndicalists was in his scepticism about what Parliament would accomplish by reform if left to carry on the fight alone, and in his distrust of a Parliamentary Labour Party dominated by middle-class ex-Liberals, pacifists, doctrinaires and humanitarian 'do-gooders.' And like the syndicalists he felt that some sort of major shake-up was required. 'I do not believe that a change of society is possible without a show-down,' he said, and in the period between 1920 and 1926 he certainly thought a show-down inevitable.

In 1940, Beaverbrook said to Churchill, 'Bevin is the most

powerful man in your Cabinet,' going on to say that he accumulated power, without knowing what to do with it. This was untrue of Ernest in 1940, but it was true of him in 1926. Though he foresaw the General Strike and to some extent prepared for it, he did not have a clear idea of what the strike was meant to achieve and certainly did not consider the implications of victory.

After the strike, it was a different matter. Ernest faced the implications of the defeat and, more to the point, faced what would have been the implications of a victory, if it had taken place. He saw now that whatever the unions might say by way of disclaiming any attempt to interfere with, challenge or threaten the State – to act politically – beyond a certain point the most genuinely conceived industrial action became a political, indeed, constitutional, affair. Ernest had the advantage of emerging from defeat absolved of the charge of treachery and/or cowardice which many trade unionists fastened on their leaders. Hostile newspapers agreed that he was the only trade union leader to have covered himself with credit – largely because of the skill and energy with which he had set about the organisation of the strike once it had started. His colleagues on the General Council admired the way he had faced Baldwin at the 'Capitulation' meeting.

After 1926, Ernest made up his mind that co-operation with the capitalists was essential. As Alan Bullock says in the first volume of his biography, this is the key to the pattern of Bevin's activities over the next ten years: participation in the Mond-Turner talks, an attempt to improve industrial relations on the basis that both unions and employers must not think of another trial of strength; the setting-up of the Economic Committee of the General Council; membership of the famous Macmillan Committee on finance and industry; membership of a Government mission of big business men to the United States.

Unions as Core of Movement

Just as Ernest saw the need to get closer to the capitalists, he saw the corresponding need to get closer to the Labour Party in general and to the Parliamentary Party in particular. He was prepared to work with them, if they would understand that the real basis of the power of the Labour Movement was the trade unions.

It was not the capacity of the unions for self-sacrifice which – in Ernie's view – made them the core and strength of the Labour Movement. He believed that their corporate wisdom, so to speak, was superior to that of the Socialist doctrinaires. He believed that they had better political judgment. He warned the Labour leaders not to enter a coalition with Lloyd George in 1917. They ignored his advice, and came to repent it. When a group of Labour leaders, including Ramsay MacDonald, Bertrand Russell and others, met at Leeds in 1917 to hail the Russian Revolution, Ernest called them 'fatuous.'

More important, Bevin and Citrine, and the T.U.C. generally, refused in 1931 to accept the analysis of the crisis with which MacDonald and Snowden presented them. Convinced that the crisis had come upon the country because British banks had been caught short through over-investing in Germany, the funds being borrowed largely from France and the United States, Bevin refused to believe that cuts in wages would do the job. (And he was proved right.) He thought the unions knew better than the Parliamentary leaders what the facts of life were.

The Attack on Lansbury

Bevin's attitude to the Labour Movement comes out in its crudest and simplest form in the episode for which he has been most criticised – his devastating attack on George Lansbury at the Labour Party Conference in the Dome, Brighton, in 1935.

The situation was dramatic. George Lansbury was the undisputed leader of the party, and though he had been unwell, and was very old, he still had tremendous moral authority and prestige. By this time, the party had, at any rate, accepted the idea that sanctions were to be used against Italy, though they had not thrashed out the question of whether these should be supported, if necessary, by armed force. George Lansbury got up and made a speech in which he said that though he was the leader of the party, in conscience he was still against the use of force. He made a most moving speech, perhaps a classic exposition of the Christian and idealist core of Labour aspirations. He was applauded to the echo. Many men wept.

Before the cheering had died down, Ernest Bevin rose from his seat and went up to the platform, as usual rolling gently from side to side like a ship. His speech was typically harsh, realistic and unadorned. Beginning slowly, it became more and more tense, until finally he was hammering away at Lansbury with a sledge-hammer.

Feared a New Treachery

Bevin's anger sprang from something much deeper than anything going on in the conference. In the first place, he feared another act of treachery on the part of the leadership of the Movement. He had never forgotten MacDonald. Now he feared Lansbury was going to upset things. Bevin despised leaders who wanted to cling on to their conscience with one hand and to power with the other. This was how he saw George Lansbury behaving.

He also saw in Lansbury the good-natured but woolly-minded pacifist who in the last ditch, if not the earlier ones, would not have the guts to use force. He despised his attitude as unrealistic and feared it might undermine the Movement. Thirdly, he saw the hand of the 'intellectuals' in this.

'Intellectual' was a very flexible term with Ernest, and he was inclined to use it as an opprobrious epithet for anybody he happened not to like. But in his stricter moments it had to do with doctrinaire characters of middle-class background from the universities. He sometimes spoke of the 'university complex' which bedevilled the party from time to time. The 'university complex' had led to far too few trade union leaders being included in the Governments of 1924 and 1931.

Whether Lansbury would have been defeated at Brighton if Bevin had not spoken in the way he did is open to discussion. But as things turned out, he could not go on, and he resigned on October 8.

I have heard it said that had George Lansbury's resignation not taken place until after the General Election, only a few weeks away, Herbert Morrison, who had been out of the House since 1931, would have had strong claims to succeed him. Bullock seems to take this view. Personally, I do not think so.

I do not know what would have happened if Morrison, instead of me, had become head of the party. After Ernest had found that the fact that I was middle-class had not given me a 'university complex' we got on well. He and Herbert did not.

Two Views on Nationalisation

Ernest Bevin and Herbert Morrison, though they had both come from working-class backgrounds, and had shown the same strength of determination and mental ability in climbing to positions of great honour and power and usefulness, had not a great deal in common. In the first place, Ernest's power had been for and through the trade union movement – an industrial power. Herbert Morrison's had come through his work in local government and the position he created for himself at the head of the L.C.C.

Both men knew a great deal about organisation, but whereas Ernest thought mainly in terms of, so to speak, internal organisation – the organisation of a body bound together by the same single interest – Herbert Morrison had much more experience of government, of genuinely public affairs, of handling things so that enemies as well as supporters could live together with a sense of benefit.

This, I think, much affected their attitude to nationalisation. Ernest, influenced no doubt by a certain residue from his syndicalist days, always favoured the idea of workers being directly represented on the boards that ran nationalised industries. Herbert Morrison, on the contrary, believed boards should represent the public. The views clashed in 1931, when Herbert Morrison proposed the establishment of the London Passenger Transport Board. Their views on nationalisation were in conflict throughout the thirties. Morrison's ultimately prevailed.

Bullock thinks there was some personal feeling between them over this. Others attribute their incompatibility to the fact that Ernest, conscious of the importance to him, as a Labour Party leader, of his own power (based on the unions), resented Morrison as a man who also had a power of his own, though in his case based on the London Labour Party. In my view, however, the fact that they never got on was due to Ernie's distrust of Herbert as 'a slick wire-puller.'

Two Egotists

In view of Ernest's prejudices, it is curious that he was so close in his prime to 'intellectuals' like Stafford Cripps. Earlier on he had a great deal against Stafford, and he was furious with him for taking the Lansbury line, more or less, in 1935. During the Labour Government, however, he and Stafford hit it off very well. Both were West Countrymen – both pronounced 'tooth' so that 'oo' was as in 'book' – and loved the countryside. Both were men of integrity. Both, of course, were tremendous egotists – Ernest having the egoism of the artist, Stafford the egoism of the altruist. Stafford thought well enough of Ernest to suggest to him that he would make a better Prime Minister than I would in 1948. Ernest did not reciprocate this compliment.

My relationship with Ernest Bevin was the deepest of my political life. I was very fond of him, and I understand that he was fond of me. I do not know what influence our friendship, our relationship, had on the affairs of the Labour Party or on the country. We had certain things in common, however, which, I think, happened to correspond to the mutual needs and strengths of the Labour Party and the trade union movement.

Driving Force

Bevin knew that, like him, I was not a pacifist. I was not a working man, but I had lived and worked amongst the workers for several years in Limehouse. I had recoiled from the treachery of our leaders in 1931, and would have resisted the development of any other would-be Messianic figure like MacDonald. I believed that the driving force of the Labour Movement, its power, its core, came from the trade unions. It was my view that the purpose of a Labour Prime Minister was to work for the common man – not the little man, but the man that is in all of us – irrespective of class and income.

Ernest, on the other hand, came to see that because a man had been to public school it did not mean that he was on the other side of a hill. As the years went by he saw more and more of the foolishness that loyal trade unionists can sometimes display, and more of the loyalty of Labour supporters among the professional middle-classes. Ernest certainly knew that I would give up being leader at any time this seemed in the interest of the party, and I think this appealed to him. I also think he liked the fact that I didn't talk much.

The main thing that Bevin did for the Labour Movement was to create and harness power for it, and by constantly stating the trade unions' point of view, to keep the Labour Party's feet on the ground. For the trade union movement he defended the right of independent collective bargaining even when a Labour Government was in power. As I have said, he was a stabiliser rather than a rudder or a propeller; on the whole, stabilisers in politics are perhaps the rarer.

22

An Unextinguished Flame

To-day Lord Samuel celebrates his ninetieth birthday and his many friends will be congratulating him. There are two survivors of the Government which resulted from the great Liberal victory of 1906, Sir Winston Churchill and Lord Samuel. They are two eminent Victorians, links with the political world of Gladstone and Disraeli. I recall them both as young under-secretaries; now they are elder statesmen.

How different the two men are, Sir Winston pugnacious, daring, throwing himself wholeheartedly into whatever party he adorns at the time. Lord Samuel, the embodiment of compromise, a born mediator. Both types are needed in our political life. It is characteristic of them both that in 1926, when the Miners' Strike merged into the General Strike, Sir Winston ran the violently partisan *British Gazette* while Lord Samuel, having presided over a Royal Commission on the Mines, helped to settle the General Strike.

Best of Both

It is not that one man has courage and force, the other brains and generosity. Both have plenty of these qualities, but their temperaments select which should predominate. Fortunately our British tradition makes it possible to get the best out of both kinds of men. Happy is the man who lives at the time when his particular qualities are most needed. Sir Winston and the country were fortunate in having him in the Second World War. Lord Samuel, who has all the qualities of a great peace-time Minister, was not so fortunate. Had he been born a few years earlier, he might have been a dominant member in the Liberal Government of 1906. Born ten years later, he might have played a great part in the Labour Party. As it was he came to the plenitude of his powers in the twilight of the Liberal Party. Thus his great administrative ability was unused for many years.

Old men's connections with the past go very far back. I recall Sir Winston's proud boast that he had been in the Government with a man who had been in Lord Palmerston's Cabinet – and Palmerston was in office during the Peninsular War. I remember Lord Samuel telling me that when at Balliol he wrote an essay on the Letters of Junius for Jowett in which he opposed the theory that they were written by Sir Philip Francis. 'You may be right,' said Jowett. 'I remember a friend of Francis telling me that he was far too conceited a man to have done anything anonymously.' That carries us back to the eighteenth century.

Lord Samuel grew up in the optimistic Victorian atmosphere before doubts of the triumphant march of progress had come to dim the vision. He has retained a mild cheerfulness about where the world is heading. He is a philosopher, but how eminent in that domain of thought I lack qualifications to judge. But above all he is a Liberal, and a Liberal because Liberalism to him is a constructive policy, something positive, not a convenient way of escaping responsibility by negations.

Into Politics

In his undergraduate days he was a Conservative, but an unusually open-minded one. It took some courage in those days to invite a dangerous firebrand such as Keir Hardie to Oxford. He became a Liberal after electioneering for his brother in an L.C.C. election. Canvassing in Whitechapel opened the eyes of this well-to-do young man to the conditions in which people lived in East London. It lit in him a steady flame for social justice never to be extinguished, and he decided to enter politics.

Taking office in his early thirties he did good service in the Home Office. The setting up of the probation service and of juvenile courts was just his line of country, but the First World War came and put him in less suitable circumstances for developing his bent. He had served as Postmaster-General, President of the Local Government Board and Home Secretary.

When Lloyd George ousted Asquith he was offered the War Office, but his essential integrity revolted against the atmosphere of intrigue. 'I greatly dislike the way the change has come about and to take office in Lloyd George's Government would be to condone it,' he said.

Party in Disarray

After World War One, he became High Commissioner for Palestine and presided over the early days of the Jewish National Home. The lot of the man who tries to hold the scales of justice is not easy. The Arabs regarded him with enmity, while his advocacy of a bi-national State lost him the sympathy of the Zionists. Returning to British politics he found the Liberal Party in disarray. He played a considerable part in forming the Coalition Government of 1931, taking office for the last time, but soon found that the pretended agreement to differ on the Free Trade issue quite unworkable and crossed the floor to lead the rather forlorn little band of Liberals who refused to become, under the name of National Liberals, a mere appendage to the Tory Party. He carried on the thankless task of leading a small third party, first in the Commons and then in the Lords, with great devotion.

Lord Samuel has often been accused of sitting on the fence and of allowing his desire for compromise to carry him into the region of ineffectiveness, but this criticism is inevitably levied against mediators who take the middle of the road, and view with cool detachment the hot-gospellers on either side.

The House of Lords is peculiarly fitted for men of his temperament and he holds a high position there. Perhaps still the most effective speaker in the House, he is heard with great respect. He is honoured as a man who has never been self-seeking, a man of high integrity and mature wisdom. Long may he be spared to us.

23

Bevan as Hero

A biographer should be in sympathy with his subject, but not a hero-worshipper. If he is, the hero must always be right and his opponents wrong. This is the case with Mr. Michael Foot and his biography of Aneurin Bevan.*

A pity, because much of this book is extraordinarily good and throws much light on one of the most colourful personalities of recent political life. The picture of the environment in which Bevan grew up is admirable – the family life in Tredegar, the dreamy bookish father and the extremely competent mother who kept the home together. Then the descriptions of early friendships, a brilliant young man with wide ranging interests and inquiring mind tramping the hills with a congenial companion, discussing everything under the sun, or sitting alone digesting his voluminous reading.

Two disabilities

Apart from one or two errors which will be corrected, no doubt – 1922 on page 27 must be a misprint for 1912 – and occasional meaningless sentences like, 'He became a puritan sensualist, or, maybe, a sensual puritan,' the first fifth of the book is outstanding. Foot is equally successful in a later chapter in describing the home life of the Bevans and the curious friendships that Aneurin had with sundry young Tories and Lord Beaverbrook, though one may question whether he would have been

*Aneurin Bevan Vol. 1, 1897–1945, by Michael Foot. MacGibbon and Kee, 1962.

equally tolerant had these associations been made by anyone not belonging to the so-called Left.

The book suffers from two disabilities. Michael Foot followed Bevan as M.P. for Ebbw Vale, and to expect any criticism of his predecessor is asking the acolyte to criticise the god in whose temple he serves. The other disability is that Mr. Foot himself is at odds with the party to which he belongs. He, like Bevan, has had the whip withdrawn, and one is doubtful sometimes as to how far he is concentrating on writing a life of Bevan and how far he is concerned to defend his own attitudes in politics.

The 1931 crisis

Take 1931. He skates gently over MacDonald's role in the crisis. Foot seems to want MacDonald blamed as little as possible so that the party as a whole can get a wigging. Talking of leadership of the Labour Party immediately after the crisis, and the 'spirit of comradeship' developed in the attack on Tory unemployment policy, he grants that this 'was probably the happiest collaboration that Labour had ever known at the top.' However, George Lansbury is the 'Mark Antony,' Cripps is the 'Octavius,' and I the 'Lepidus' of the outfit.

Poor old George. Anybody less like Antony I never knew. Stafford had not the slightest resemblance to Octavius. As for me, whenever I appear in the narrative it seems to be to illustrate the point that I was never any use at anything.

As well as having too much Foot in it, the book is much too long. The scale in itself makes for misleading impressions. For instance, 104 pages out of 510 are headed 'The Fight with Churchill.' This amount of space and emphasis is ludicrously disproportionate to its real importance. Between June, 1941, and July, 1942, Bevan was no more than an irritant, a minor annoyance.

His good sense

Much of the impression of Bevan which emerges is well done. The skilled craftsman working the long hours of that time in the pit and in his spare time inspiring forward movements in the neighbourhood – very interestingly described. Foot goes on to trace Bevan's entrance into public life – Town Council, Board of Guardians and the City Council. Also very interesting. I was surprised to learn how long it took for Labour to capture these bodies, much longer than in East London. The story unfolds informatively until the young Bevan, seeking the source of power, finally becomes a Member of Parliament under the very exceptional circumstances of ousting the sitting Member, a fellow miner.

His attitude to the Communists was characteristic of his strong good sense. He accepted what was valid in the doctrines of Marx, but never fell for Communist dogma. Bevan was never a dogmatist, though he often sounded as if he were. He loved poetry and nature too much and his range of human interests was too wide. He would never have succumbed to a narrow materialist creed. Foot has described all this faithfully and well.

Too much hindsight

Unfortunately he goes off the rails again when he comes to deal with Bevan's clashes with the party leaders over, for instance, the Popular Front. It is not that he is over-sympathetic to Bevan, but that the case for the leaders is not put. They were very conscious of how many democratic socialist parties on the Continent had been given the kiss of death by the Communist Party. It was impossible for members of the executive to ignore Bevan and Cripps while enforcing – as was their duty – the rule on minor offenders in local parties. The refusal of the Labour Party to be beguiled into joining the Popular Front was fully justified when British Communists fell into line with the Russians in joining the Fascists in the Molotov-Ribbentrop Pact.

Of Bevan's views on the conduct of the war, the book does not give a very satisfactory picture. Throughout several of its pages one cannot make out when it is Bevan and when it is Foot attacking the Government's high strategy. Bevan and/or Foot seem quite unable to understand why Churchill and Alanbrooke should have had any doubts as to the Russians' powers of resistance. This would only wash now if Bevan/Foot could have anticipated the great help the Russians received from Hitler's assuming the position of war lord and causing the disaster of Stalingrad. Too much hindsight. Also, of course, genuine ignorance.

According to Foot, Bevan's motive in criticising Winston was that 'the House of Commons must be Winston Churchill's master.' I doubt if Bevan's behaviour in the House at that time was ever governed by so systematic a purpose. In the House he was often carried away by his own indisputable powers of speech. He loved to use this gift, and frequently presented ammunition to his enemies.

Bugbear of the Tories

Foot's book concludes with an account of the termination of the Coalition Government. His approach to the matter is indicated by the title of his chapter: 'The Scruff of their Necks.' The Coalition ended, he says, with Ernest Bevin and me being 'hauled out by the scruff of their necks.' In fact, Bevin and I disagreed with some of my Labour colleagues not about leaving the Coalition, but about when the election should be held. The Japanese war was still on and we were advised it might last another six months. We were also against having a snap election in July which we thought was not fair to the Servicemen. We therefore hoped for a continuation of the National Government until October. There was never any question of either Bevin or myself being opposed to Labour fighting the election on its own or favouring a post-election Coalition. Foot's description of these events is lively, but leaves much to be desired.

A word now on Bevan. He could have been a great parliamentary orator but he did not always act on the principle that a great orator must always try to persuade. Bevan *could* persuade, if he tried, but too often he flew into abuse of his opponents and consequently put people off, even when his case was sound. 'I *love* being the bugbear of the Tories,' he told me once. I said, 'You can't be the bugbear of the Tories and be regarded as a statesman.'

When he wanted to, he displayed real gifts as a conciliator, which was why I asked him, on the foundation of the Labour Cabinet in 1945, to take the Ministry of Health. (It is not true that this was Bevin's idea.) He was also an excellent administrator when he was interested enough to get on with the job. At the Ministry of Health he rendered great service.

I found Aneurin Bevan both likeable and attractive. He could be arrogant, but that never worried me, though I disliked the way, when still a brash young man, he would speak contemptuously to party veterans who had been slogging unrewarded before he was born. Though basically of great generosity, in heat he showed narrowness which led to faulty judgments. For instance, I think he believed for years that people would not fight in any war except a class-war, not realising the Tories loved their country as well as their class.

Natural leader

I admired much about him to the extent that I thought he would have been a natural leader of the Labour Party if one was sure he would learn to keep his temper. Far from standing in his way, I tried to bring him on. I said to him when I had made him Minister of Health, 'You are the youngest member of the Cabinet. Now it's up to you. The more you can learn, the better.' I made it clear he was starting with me with a clean sheet. Later, when it was clear he had laid fine foundations for Health, I thought it would be good for him to have a change of office to widen his experience. I suggested the Colonial Office. He said clearly that he wanted to stay where he was as there was important work still to do.

In 1951 a new Foreign Secretary was required to replace Bevin. Among others I asked Bevan whom he thought would make a good Foreign Secretary. I can't remember what he said, but he certainly did not ask for the job himself; and he did not indicate that he wanted it – contrary to what has frequently been said since. I told him it was time he had a change. The Ministry of Labour was one of the key jobs. Hitherto Ernest Bevin's influence had still been strong in industrial matters, but now we needed a new force there. I offered it to Bevan and he accepted it without demur.

Patience is essential

If we had won the 1955 election, and I had continued as Prime Minister, and he had started to behave then as he did in late 1957, I would have tried him as Foreign Secretary. Not as Chancellor of the Exchequer. I firmly hold the view that it is necessary for the Chancellor of the Exchequer to have considerable technical economic knowledge of the kind that Cripps and Gaitskell had. This is not because the technical knowledge is all that important, but because unless Chancellors have it, they will be in the hands of their permanent officials.

Whether Bevan would have made a great Prime Minister is doubtful. He had many of the rare attributes, but he did not suffer fools gladly enough. A Prime Minister, especially in peacetime, must be most patient. He cannot afford to be autocratic. He must not talk too much in Cabinet. This habit nearly wrecked Winston even at the height of his power. Nye may well have foundered on this dangerous rock.

24

Courageous Intellectual

If John Strachey were a typical sample of the intellectual in politics, we could do with a few more. He could run a Government department well and used his intellectual powers, not to by-pass problems, but to try to solve them.

Not sufficiently easy in personal relations and man-management to make a Prime Minister, perhaps, though he was not a man who made enemies. In the thirties he said and did things I did not care for, politically speaking. But as a human being I found him no less likeable then than I did in the days of his maturity.

His background – Eton, Oxford and a somewhat over-specialised set of relatives – had increased his desire to think but had not given him enough to think about. In the early thirties, like so many of us, he became fed to the teeth with Ramsay MacDonald. But for him only the two political extremes seemed sufficiently different from Ramsay to be worth examining.

Feet on ground

Vanity, myopia and fear of looking foolish often slow down the rate at which a man will publicly admit his error. Strachey was never afraid of looking a fool, and therefore could travel back to common sense fast. His wartime years in the R.A.F. were very good for him. They taught him about men and matters he might not otherwise have met. From then on he always had his feet on the ground.

Certain of this, I made him Under-Secretary of State for Air in 1945. It was a tougher assignment than it looked. He did so well I decided to try him as Minister of Food in 1946 – a very sticky wicket. He showed himself a good administrator and a man of courage.

Then came the groundnuts scheme. It was an imaginative plan. He worked on it down to the last detail and took the very best advice from the leaders of the trade, who all thought it was 'on.' Looking back on it, I think his only mistake was to go in on a large scale, instead of starting with a pilot scheme.

Strachey was a hard worker, with the intellectual humility and fearlessness to face his own ignorance. He never worked just for the sake of working, but in everything he set himself to do, he shirked nothing. He took trouble, an excellent virtue in politicians, who, knowing the speed with which things change, may be tempted to take short cuts or avoid chores.

I would like to have seen Strachey as Minister of Defence in the next Labour Government, and I think he would have been outstanding. He had equipped himself to talk equally cogently to experts and to laymen. Britain would have had a Minister who had pondered defence as a whole, and would act only in terms of that total conception.

Useful on finance

He would have been good in Cabinet. He wouldn't have talked too much, and would have put up extremely able papers. He might also have been very useful on other matters, such as finance.

Strachey made many valuable contributions to our thinking about the problems of our times. His book on 'The End of Empire' was balanced, fair, profound and realistic. His last book on the problem of survival in an age of nuclear weapons was the most informed and systematic discussion of the subject that anybody in politics has personally undertaken, and certainly the most logical. Few men are intellectually and politically equipped to tackle these vast and complex technical problems.

The second part of his book deals with the related problem of World Government. There are many who believe in, and work for, the cause of World Government who, like me, do not agree with some of his views as to how it is to be most expeditiously established. This in no way diminishes the value of his book.

Indeed his critics owe a special debt to him for stimulating them to further thought.

All in all it can be said that even if he were to be judged by his writings alone he would have rendered great service to his party, his country and his fellow men. John's death is a loss to all three.

25
She Made Things Hum

Nancy Astor could be as bold as brass but she was in fact a kind and compassionate woman with, especially where women were concerned, a great sense of justice. She was no respecter of persons, and would take you down a peg as soon as look at you, but not if you were getting a raw deal or were down on your luck.

Good souls, men or women, rich or poor, had nothing to fear from her. She admired goodness – 'I'm not good myself, but I only admire good people,' she used to say – and it brought out something protective in her. She could scent selfishness a mile off. Hypocrites and climbers were advised to give her a wide berth. One remark from her could puncture a reputation, and she never bothered about who was listening.

In the House of Commons she said a number of foolish things from time to time, but so have Cabinet Ministers. On the whole she was a tremendous asset. Her very presence, as our first woman Member, was a blow for egalitarianism in general, and as long as she had any breath in her she was ready to speak up for the better and more equal treatment of women. Her attitude to nursery schools, which she did so much to promote, was typical of her: she wanted them not only because they were good for the children, but because they took some of the burdens off working-class mothers.

I wasn't in sympathy with some of her views on foreign policy in the later thirties, but they came from an earnest wish to prevent a war, and if they misjudged Hitler's intentions they were sincere and humane. Millions of people shared them. Though she called herself a Conservative – the Conservatives called her everything – she was in many ways on our side on domestic issues, and

145

reformers of all parties owe a lot to her. Party lines meant little to her.

Funds and work

Her husband, Waldorf – a fine man – I never regarded as a Conservative. I thought him very much with us. They were both exceptionally public-spirited, and were ready not only to donate funds but to work themselves really hard. But her most valuable work was to make it possible, often behind the scenes, for able and worthy people, welfare workers and social reformers, to get a hearing and a chance to *act*. She was among the impresarios of the Welfare State.

As for her unique personality, Nancy frequently brought Queen Elizabeth I to my mind. She, too, had the heart and courage of a man, had a tongue like a whip, was unpredictable and wilful, yet had great funds of feeling, which often showed in almost childlike tenderness. They would both behave like men, with great shrewdness and determination, but, when it suited them, fall back on their femininity without scruple. They would rant or sob to get their way, and watch you out of the corner of an eye all the time. You never knew quite where you were with either of them, but they knew where they were with you.

Wealth and power, though she had them and used them, did not mean much to Nancy except in terms of people. She loved company, the more varied the better, and she could exchange compliments or insults on equal terms with dukes or dockers. She was larger than life. She had values, personal as well as social, and the fire and drive to project them. People like Nancy Astor, quite apart from their good works, are atmospheric. They make things hum. One does not see many people of her calibre in public life today, which is a pity.

26

Toynbee Hall Looks to the Future

Eighty years ago Toynbee Hall was founded by Canon Barnett, the first settlement, since copied elsewhere at home and in the United States. I can recall attending as an undergraduate at Oxford more than 60 years ago a meeting addressed by Mr. Asquith, as he then was, and Mr. C. F. G. Masterman for support of Toynbee Hall. The appeal was then mainly for personal service, for the buildings and equipment were adequate and up to date.

A few years later I went to live in Limehouse and in 1910 went to Whitechapel to be secretary of the settlement. Canon and Mrs. Barnett and some of the earliest residents were still active then. I became fully acquainted with all the work carried on both individually and collectively by the residents of Toynbee. Many men of distinction such as the late Lord Beveridge worked there and many social experiments were originated there. Now a new appeal is being launched.

Mass of Legislation

Since the settlement was founded many changes have taken place in Britain, especially in East London. Legislative and administrative reforms have changed the nature of the problems which faced the early settlers. The Trades Boards Act, the decasualization of dock labour and the mass of legislation which has brought about what is called the welfare state have altered the economic position of the people of Stepney.

Many advances pioneered by Toynbee Hall have been generalized. For instance its educational activities which bulked so large in early days have now been taken over by the L.C.C. Equally important has been the physical change in the neighbourhood resulting from two world wars and the passage of time. Thousands of old slum dwellings were destroyed in the Second World War. But although many new blocks of flats have been built and although the population has been halved the problem of housing in Stepney remains one of real gravity. Much good work has been done by the London County Council and the Stepney Borough Council. Toynbee Hall itself was badly blitzed and time has rendered obsolete much of the surviving buildings.

Extended Education

It is right and natural that the activities of a settlement should change with the times. No longer is a settlement an adventure into unknown territory inhabited by an entirely different stratum of society.

Extended education and the advances of working people into the field of government, local and national, have altered the relationship between classes. Nevertheless there is still work to be done although the mass poverty of former days has practically passed away.

Despite Old Age Pensions and the abolition of the Poor Law, there is still the problem of the aged. Despite the rebuilding of much of the area there is still much bad housing. There is need for the promotion of neighbourliness. Indeed with the old slums has passed away a good deal of the cheerful social life of poor streets as I knew it. Blocks of modern flats are, I think, less conducive to community life. Despite all the excellent work done by girls' and boys' clubs the problem of young people is, I think, more difficult than in earlier days. There is, too, the problem of racial admixture.

Fine Tradition

Stepney has always had a number of residents from countries inhabited by non-white peoples and has a fine tradition of tolerance, but the position still requires careful watching and active work to avoid incidents such as have occurred in other districts.

I have no fear that there will be any lack of young men from the universities to carry on the old traditions and to bring to new activities the spirit of unselfish service, but the present appeal sponsored by many distinguished people is for funds to replace, renew and rebuild Toynbee Hall as the basis for the social work of the residents.

I have said that the housing problem is still acute in Stepney. Toynbee must begin by setting its own house in order. Buildings which in their day registered a big advance are now obsolete, some even condemned. Part of the task for which money is required is to develop, enlarge and modernize the tenement flats for old people and others in urgent need.

New Building

A new building is required to house the Warden and six young men. A new venture will be a new residential block for 12 young men from East London as part of an approach to dealing with the youth problem.

I have mentioned other spheres of work. It is of the essence of settlement work that varieties of personal service are given by residents besides what is done in the settlement itself. I have said that I believe that residents from the universities will come to the settlement as in the past, but there must be a settlement to which they can come.

I might adapt the famous words of Sir Winston Churchill, 'Give us the tools and we will carry on the job.' Carry on, not finish, for wars finish, but there is no foreseeable end to the campaign for social advance.

27

In the Driver's Seat

Having won the election, Harold Wilson's first big job was to form his Cabinet. In a way it is more difficult than winning the election, because in choosing his Cabinet the Prime Minster is on his own, and carries the can for his mistakes. Once the appointments have been made, he is going to be stuck with them for a considerable period. If some of the choices soon look unsatisfactory, he cannot start sacking them right away. Moreover, he must give each man a chance, and stand the racket while he improves, grows to the job. If the Prime Minister starts pushing his departmental heads, the morale of the Cabinet as a whole will suffer.

The qualities of the ideal Cabinet Minister are: judgment, strength of character, experience of affairs, and an understanding of ordinary people.

Judgment is necessary because the Cabinet is the instrument by which decisions are reached with a view to action, and decisions stem from judgment. A Cabinet is not a place for eloquence – one reason why good politicians are not always good Cabinet Ministers. It is judgment which is needed to make important decisions on imperfect knowledge in a limited time. Men either have it, or they haven't. They can develop it, if they have it; but cannot acquire it if they haven't.

Strength of character is required to stand up to criticism from other Cabinet members, pressure from outside groups, and the advice of civil servants.

It is also necessary when policies, on which the Cabinet has agreed, are going through the doldrums, or are beginning to fail. A man of character will neither be, nor seem to be, bowed down by this. Nor will he be blown about by 'every wind of vain doctrine.'

Experience

General experience of affairs is most valuable; experience of organisations, of groups and societies, or of business and industry. (Businessmen, however, while good in Cabinet, may not be good in the House of Commons, not used to explaining and defending their courses of action to the public; this is essential, and is where men like Woolton failed.) Cabinet Ministers are no good if they cannot put their stuff over in the House – sell it, explain it. (That is where that good man Creech-Jones failed.)

Young men cannot be expected to have much experience, but this need not exclude them from the Cabinet. Harold Wilson was in the Cabinet at the age of 30, and was a model of what at that age a Cabinet member can be. He had considerable knowledge of a particular field, stuck to it, and didn't talk too much, did not try to impress, was not afraid of his seniors, was on top of his civil servants, and when he spoke did so with authority. Gordon Walker was also in for a short time. I can give him good marks, too – reasonable, good at putting a case, vigorous, on top of his civil servants; he shut up as soon as possible.

It is most important that the Cabinet discussion should take place, so to speak, at a higher level than the information and opinions provided by the various departmental briefs. A collection of departmental Ministers does not make a Cabinet. A Cabinet consists only of responsible human beings. And it is their thinking and judgment in broad terms that make a Government tick, not arguments about the recommendations of civil servants. It is interesting to note that quite soon a Cabinet begins to develop a group personality. The role of the Prime Minister is to cultivate this, if it is efficient and right-minded; to do his best to modify it, if it is not.

While a collection of departmental heads mouthing their top civil servants' briefs is unsatisfactory, a collection of Ministers who are out of touch with administration tends to be unrealistic. And a Minister who has an itch to run everybody else's department as well as, or in preference to, his own is just a nuisance. Some men will be ready to express a view about everything. They should be discouraged. If necessary, I would shut them up. Once is enough. Ernie Bevin held forth on a variety of subjects, but Ernie had an extraordinary variety of practical knowledge.

Wisdom

It is a curious thing that nearly every Cabinet throws up at least one man, whether he is a departmental Minister or not, of whom a newcomer might ask, 'What is *he* doing here?' He is there because he is wise. You will hear a junior Cabinet Minister being told by the Prime Minister, perhaps, 'If you are going to do that, old boy, you would be well advised to have a talk with X.'

The ability to talk attractively in Cabinet is not essential. Being able to put a case clearly and succinctly and simply is what counts. The Cabinet is certainly not the place for rhetoric. Though an excellent head of department and a conciliator of genius, Nye Bevan used to talk a bit too much occasionally. Usually he was extremely good, often wise, and sometimes extremely wise; '75 per cent of political wisdom is a sense of priorities,' I remember him saying once – an admirable remark, and good advice for Cabinet Ministers.

The occasions when he talked too much were when he got excited because he felt that our policies were falling short of the pure milk of the word. This goes for most such interruptions, and a Prime Minister should try to avoid these time-consuming expressions of guilt – or electoral fear – by trying to reassure from time to time the pure in heart who feel the Government is backsliding.

However, you cannot choose people according to what makes an ideal Cabinet Minister. In the first place, you must choose people with regard to keeping balance within the party. This need not be overdone. It is a matter of democratic common sense, not of craven below-the-scenes manipulation. It would not do to have all trade unionists in a Labour Cabinet, or all constituency members, or all middle-class intellectuals, or all ornaments of the Co-operative Party. Some working-class trade unionists are in fact honorary members of the intelligentsia – Nye again – while I have known upper-class intellectuals try desperately to behave like heavy-handed sons of toil – Charlie Trevelyan, for instance [*the late Sir Charles Trevelyan, elder brother of the historian and a former Education Minister*].

Personality

A Prime Minister must also bear in mind the party's view of a man's capacity, because this could be crucial in getting through unpalatable policies fast. But he must also have his own view of him, and not part with it easily. This means sitting long hours in the House of Commons, seeing how your own party behaves to him and, also important, how the Opposition behaves to him. Nobody at his peak was more powerful than Baldwin in his Cabinet. Baldwin sat for hours listening in the House. When Lloyd George stopped going to the House, his grip on his Cabinet weakened.

Another factor which limits a Premier's freedom of choice is personality. I have already written in The Observer that Herbert Morrison and Ernie Bevin did not hit it off together. I could not have Herbert as Leader of the House, for which he was well fitted, with Ernie also on the home front as Chancellor of the Exchequer. This was the balancing factor in Ernie getting the Foreign Office. As it happened, he proved to be a great Foreign Secretary.

Nor does a man always get the job he wants, or which you would best like him to have. I disappointed Chuter Ede, who wanted to be Minister of Education, because I wanted him for the more difficult task of Home Secretary. Chuter never complained, but just got on with it. Your two or three main jobs must go to your two or three main men. Ability is not conclusive – standing in the party must be considered. Not that men popular in the party should assume they have a predestined right to office. I do not like this Shadow Cabinet business. It may lead a man to think he is an authority on a subject and therefore a certainty for that department when the time comes. Besides, men should not be encouraged to specialise too much: there is too much of that already. The Prime Minister should be understood to be the only certainty for a job: everybody else should be ultimately at his disposal.

Ministers should not be allowed too much freedom in

appointing their deputies or junior Ministers. It makes for empire-building, and may engender yes-men. A Prime Minister may appoint a trade unionist to the No. 1 job and correct his bias or supplement his outlook by appointing a middle-class economics don as his No. 2. I would not saddle a Minister with a junior colleague he could not stand. I would weigh his views upon the subject.

The three key jobs are Foreign Secretary, Chancellor of the Exchequer, and Minister of Defence. You need big men for all three, men with brains and guts. The Foreign Secretary, above all, must be able to stand up to pressure – from members of his party, lobbies and the volume of work. He must have no favourites or *bêtes noires* among the countries of the world, and be strong enough to deal with anybody who tries to impose one on him. Diplomats are a clever lot. A Foreign Secretary need know no language except his own: Ernie Bevin didn't even bother to pronounce M. Ramadier; he always called him Remedier. But he must know what's going on.

The Chancellor must also be of strength and standing in the party, able to influence his spending Ministers and tell them where to get off. He needn't be an economic expert – the main thing is to know enough to stop economists blinding him with science.

And the Minister of Defence must be neutral to all services and show it – not, of course, the neutrality of an all-round ignorance, but of motive. He needn't know much about war or care for it particularly.

Decisions

Too much knowledge is a dubious asset. For instance, an excellent Minister of Agriculture was Tom Williams, who was no expert at it: Tory landowners in the job have accomplished little.

The Cabinet usually meets once a week. That should be enough for regular meetings, and should be if they grasp from the start what they are there for. They should be back at their work as soon as possible and a Prime Minister should put as little as possible in their way. We started sharp at 11, and rose in time for lunch. Even in a crisis, another couple of meetings should be enough in the same week: if there is a crisis, the less talk the better.

The Prime Minister shouldn't speak too much himself in Cabinet. He should start the show or ask somebody else to do so, and then intervene only to bring out the more modest chaps who, despite their seniority, might say nothing if not asked. And the Prime Minister must sum up. Experienced Labour leaders should be pretty good at this; they have spent years attending debates at meetings of the Parliamentary Party and the National Executive, and have to sum *those* up. That takes some doing – good training for the Cabinet.

Particularly when a non-Cabinet Minister is asked to attend, especially if it is his first time, the Prime Minister may have to be cruel. The visitor may want to show how good he is, and go on too long. A good thing is to take no chance and ask him to send the Cabinet a paper in advance. The Prime Minister can then say, 'A very clear statement, Minister of —. Do you need to add anything?' in a firm tone of voice obviously expecting the answer, *No*. If somebody else looks like making a speech, it is sound to nip in with 'Has anybody any objection?' If somebody starts to ramble, a quick 'Are you *objecting*? You're not? Right. Next business,' and the Cabinet can move on.

It is essential for the Cabinet to move on, leaving in its wake a trail of clear, crisp, uncompromising decisions. This is what government is about. And the challenge to democracy is how to get it done quickly.

28
The Man I Knew

Churchill, I consider, was the greatest leader in war this country has ever known. Not the greatest warrior. As a strategist, he was not in the same class as Cromwell, and if he had ever commanded armies in the field I doubt if he would ever have been a Marlborough. But a war leader must be much more than a warrior, and do much more than make war. Above all he must stand like a beacon for his country's will to win. And give it constant voice, and translate it into action.

I rate him supreme as Britain's leader in war because he was able to solve the problem that democratic countries in total war find crucial and may find fatal: relations between the civil and military leaders. Lloyd George had an instinct that told him when the generals were doing anything wrong, but he did not have the military knowledge to tell the generals what was right. Churchill did. He did not overrule the generals. But he always had chapter and verse with which to meet their protests and to lead them to a positive course of his own.

In my view, he was a greater leader in war than Chatham because he personally made more impact on the men who fought. He had the capacity for being a symbol, a figure that meant something to the individual fighting man. As a public figure he was much more attractive, and therefore more influential, than the younger Pitt, and he set the impress of a single mind – essential when a fight is on – much more effectively on his colleagues and subordinates.

If somebody asked me what exactly Winston did to win the war, I would say, 'Talk about it.' In the Cabinet he talked about practically nothing else. After about 1942, when he and the Chiefs

157

of Staff concentrated on the running of the war, and left John Anderson and myself to deal with domestic affairs, if Winston couldn't talk about the war he would rather not talk at all. The only parts of home affairs he was interested in were those which bore upon the war effort. He took no interest in the famous White Paper on Post-War Britain. Indeed, we had some difficulty in persuading him to read it.

Monologues

Now and again he would pick up some document on home affairs in the Cabinet, take up one of the memoranda on top, or pounce on one of the minutes written half-way through it, and ask some question in the tone of a man who had read the whole thing through several times, and discovered the critical weakness in it, and was now going to hold a grand inquest.

'What about *this*!' he would say, glowering around the room. Sometimes we would have to point out to him that the passage he quoted was followed by its refutation and was not a recommendation. If he was in the mood, quite unabashed, he would try another. Or again, he might ignore our observation, and hold forth for 10 or 15 minutes about something that no longer existed.

We used to let him get it off his chest, and not interrupt – indeed, it was extremely difficult to interrupt him because not only had he no intention of stopping, but frequently he had no intention of listening. His monologues sometimes went on for very long periods indeed.

Much has been written about the way he would send out memoranda on small points of detail, which gave generals out in the field the impression, until they came to know better, that he had grasped every detail of what they were doing – and not doing. 'What are we doing about the tests for signallers on Salisbury Plain?' is the kind of flash that would go out, much to the consternation of the unfortunate recipient. It frequently created a lot of confusion, because once Winston had decided to find out what was happening about those tents the whole war effort was held up until somebody had told him.

A blazing row

Very often the only thing that Winston knew about an operation was the point of detail he had covered in his memorandum. Some of the generals out in the field thought that Winston was like Big Brother in Orwell's book, looking down on them from the wall the whole time. Now and again somebody would tumble to it that this was a trick, and, realising that Winston could not possibly know about every operation in detail, take advantage of the fact. Here Winston's colossal luck or guardian angel often intervened. For this operation would sometimes turn out to be one of the many that Winston knew from A to Z. There would be hell to pay.

What Winston really did, in my view, was to keep us all on our toes. He did very little work in the Cabinet. Churchill's Cabinets, frankly, were not good for business, but they were great fun. He kept us on our toes partly by just being Winston, and partly because he was always throwing out ideas. Some of them were not very good, and some of them were downright dangerous. But they kept coming, and they kept one going, and a lot of them were excellent.

My relations with him in Cabinet always seemed to me to be very good. He talked to me extremely frankly – more frankly, I suspect, than he talked to some of his Conservative colleagues. He did not have much use for those who had supported Neville Chamberlain. He never took it out of them, he was too good-natured and, anyway, he had too high a regard for political loyalty. What he did do, however, was to get most of these Chamberlainites at as great a distance from himself as he could, and he did it very nicely. Halifax went to the United States; Sam Hoare to Spain; Malcolm MacDonald to Canada; Harlech to South Africa; and Swinton to West Africa.

Winston and I sometimes, but not often, had a blazing row. I remember one on India, but he was quite all right next morning and indeed accepted my view. He was always smoking a cigar in the Cabinet room, and now and again he would give me one. Whether it was because at that moment I had said something he particularly approved of, or because he could no longer stand the smell of my pipe, I have never discovered. I never thought of asking him.

The only thing that Winston had against me was that I was a Socialist. He used to complain about this quite bitterly at times, but I told him there was nothing he could do about it. Whenever we got on to the subject of planning for post-war Britain, Winston was ill at ease. He always groused about my being a Socialist. Whenever a Cabinet committee put up a paper to him on anything not military or naval, he was inclined to suspect a Socialist plot. Even wartime schemes for controls and rationing used to irritate him. We could never get him to understand that these were as essential to a Conservative country at war as to a Socialist one.

He became increasingly suspicious about the possibility of the Socialists putting something over on him. He thought the Socialists were cleverer than the Tories, anyway, and this naturally only increased his apprehensions. So whenever he got wind that a report or a memorandum on something outside his ken was coming up, he would get somebody to spy out the land so that he could prepare an onslaught on our 'machinations.' Winston used to describe this artlessly as 'getting a second, highly qualified and objective opinion on the issue.' In fact, what he wanted was a hatchet job.

If Winston's greatest virtue was his compassion, his greatest weakness was his impatience. He never understood that a certain time was always bound to elapse between when you ask for something to be done and when it can be effected. He worked people terribly hard, and was inconsiderate. On the whole, he did not vent his impatience on people in bursts of temper or in bullying. But, as Alanbrooke has reported in his Diaries, he kept people working impossible hours in order that he should not have to contain himself, or defer anything that he had become enthusiastic about.

He was also a poor judge of men, and he made some curious appointments. He was always liable to take a good man from a job he was doing well and give him something to do for which he was quite unsuitable.

Winston made some good appointments, too. Many a statesman would make better appointments sometimes if he was braver about them. Winston never had a tremor in selecting a man for a job – though he hated sacking people – and considerations of party would not stop him. I remember the appointment of

Temple in 1942 as Archbishop of Canterbury. Somebody asked Winston why he had made a Socialist Archbishop of Canterbury. 'Because,' he said, 'he was the only half-crown article in a sixpenny-halfpenny bazaar.'

I've said before that Churchill was not a great parliamentarian, mainly, of course, because he was too impatient to master its procedures. He was not even a great House of Commons debater in the way that Lloyd George and Birkenhead were. His speeches were magnificent rhetorical performances, but they were too stately, too pompous, too elaborate to be ideal House of Commons stuff. It was the occasions that gave the speeches their historic quality.

I heard so many of these speeches in preparation that perhaps I am not the best judge of them. He would walk up and down the room, throwing out remarks. 'I'll go to them and tell them,' he would say, and out would come some brilliant phrases to be worked later into a speech. In my view his best speeches were those which described historical moments – a victory, such as Alamein, or a defeat, such as Dunkirk. Those speeches are unique.

Tonypandy

So far as Churchill the historian is concerned, I have always admired his prose much more than his content. It seems to me that somebody would get a curious idea of what has been going on in this country for the last 2,000 years if they had to get it all from Winston. He leaves too much of the important stuff out.

If there was one thing that marked him off from the comparable figures in history, it was his characteristic way of standing back and looking at himself – and his country – as he believed history would. He was always, in effect, asking himself, 'How will I look if I do this or that?' And 'What must Britain do now so that the verdict of history will be favourable?' All he cared about, in Britain's history, of course, were the moments when Britain was great. He was always looking around for 'finest hours,' and if one was not immediately available, his impulse was to manufacture one.

I have sometimes been asked whether, when asked to join a Government under him in 1940, I had any misgivings about serving under the man who 'sent the troops to Tonypandy.' I did not. I was convinced that, whatever happened, the war had to be won first, that Winston was the man to handle the war, and that the leaders of the Labour Party could handle Winston. I never believed that Winston had been hostile to the working classes. I did not even think that he was bitter against them during the General Strike.

Superbly lucky

If he had taken a broad view of what the Conservatives should offer the electors in 1945, he would have done considerably better. But he chose to tighten the noose which the pre-war Tories had already put around his neck. His natural combativeness led him, once the campaign had taken shape, to press on with typical Churchillian *élan* down the road to defeat. As I have said, he was not a good judge of public opinion, and I think that he was sufficiently out of date in his knowledge of the man in the street in peace-time to believe that the kind of nonsense he talked about Police State versus Conservative freedom would work.

Churchill often underestimated how much the voter was affected by bread-and-butter considerations, by fears for the security of his wife and children, health and education, and so on. But it wasn't that Winston did not care about these things. Otherwise, he could not have been Lloyd George's lieutenant and helped him build the Welfare State.

Churchill was not 'anti-Beveridge.' He kept, so to speak, pushing the Report away from him because he wanted to get on and win the war. For this reason, since Winston and the Defence Committee were concentrating on the military aspects of the war, and since, as he himself says in his War Memoirs, John Anderson, Arthur Greenwood and I looked after nearly everything else, the Labour Party was very much more equipped to put the Beveridge Report into effect.

Energy, rather than wisdom, practical judgment or vision, was his supreme qualification. For energy I do not know who will rank with him outside Napoleon, Bismarck and Lloyd George. But in Churchill's case it was poetry coupled with energy that did the trick. Energy and poetry, in my view, really sum him up.

He was, of course, above all, a supremely fortunate mortal. History set him the job that he was the ideal man to do. I cannot think of anybody in this country who has been favoured in this way so much. Winston was superbly lucky. And perhaps the most warming thing about him was that he never ceased to say so.

29

Quite Possibly a Classic

This is a very good book – quite possibly a classic. Part biography, part autobiography, part memoir of the period, in places it reads like a novel, a warm and moving account of the intimate friendship between Winston and the author, beginning when he was 32 and she was 19. What stamps it is the calibre of the writer. Violet Bonham Carter is in Winston's league. Indeed, a Prime Minister's daughter when she first met him, she could look down on him from above – a point of view not given by fate to many.

Her picture of Winston, very critical in many respects, is all the more effective for being written in a spirit of love. She gets him right, but she gets him generously. Amazing that her first book, at 78, should be so good. I wonder why she hasn't started before. Too busy talking, perhaps. This volume takes us up to 1916, and gives us a wonderful picture of Edwardian England, with its leisure, wealth and glamour, and politics run by half a dozen drawing-rooms. I saw the same England from the street corners of Limehouse; interesting to learn later what was going on at the top.

* * *

The book throws new light on many matters. Not least it has given me a rather different view of Asquith. I had always thought him a great man – of fine intellect, high principle, noble feeling – but lacking the power of decision. I now feel from reading Lady Violet that he was in fact a decisive man. What did for him was his unreadiness to believe the worst of people. He couldn't bring himself to believe Lloyd George was so deceitful and Winston so erratic. He trusted too much. He comes out of this book extremely well, and I do not think this has much to do with the author being his daughter. Kitchener comes out rather well, too. I thought him a stuffed shirt, poor fellow, but he seems to have been human. Balfour comes out rather less languid than usual, but Fisher even madder. I never thought much of John Morley: he was an old woman if ever there was one.

Apart from anything else, it is a very amusing book. Winston himself, though he comes out a giant and a genius, comes out also as distinctly comic. Quite right: he always was, knew it, and loved it. Some of Lloyd George's cracks are vintage – splendid invective against the Lords, e.g., 'An aristocracy is like cheese: the older it is the higher it becomes.' And some of the cracks against him, too: Keynes, in answer to the question 'What do you think happens to Mr Lloyd George when he is alone in the room?' replying: 'When he is alone in the room there is nobody there.'

So far as I know nobody has recorded so good a picture of Winston. Page 225, for instance – an acute analysis of his peculiar genius. 'A man's life,' he once wrote, 'must be nailed to a cross either of thought or action,' but his own life belied this judgment. Lady Violet says:–

> *Throughout his life he has refused to accept the ruling of the modern world that he must either plan or perform, conceive or execute. ... I always thought, and often told him, that he had been born out of due season, that he should rightly have belonged to an age in which thought and action were a combined operation and not alternative functions each allotted to specialists in their own spheres. But with the Second World War, when every decision was a deed, he entered into his double heritage.*

Dead right, and beautifully put.

The book brings out his peculiarities as well as his powers. At 32 he had never heard of Keats's 'Ode to a Nightingale' and thought that Blake, the eighteenth-century poet, was the same chap as the seventeenth-century admiral. Years later, even after Lady Violet had got some poetry into his head, he hadn't read a word of Tennyson. There are wonderful anecdotes about his eccentric way of playing bridge and the consternation he caused his bridge-playing private secretaries: 'But First Lord,' squeaked the affronted Masterton, 'you discarded the knave. ....' Winston: 'The cards I throw away are not worthy of observation or I should not discard them. It is the cards I *play* on which you should concentrate your attention.' There are wonderful stories about him and Lloyd George, especially when Winston became First Lord and promptly lost all interest in the Welfare State – 'He declaimed about his blasted ships for a whole morning,' Lloyd George said bitterly. 'He forgets that most of us live on land.' What Lloyd George and he had in common, of course, was an insatiable appetite for talking politics. But even L.G. found Winston's appetite surprising. He told Lord Riddell that at his wedding Winston started talking politics to him in the vestry.

The greatest fascination of the book is what it tells us of the author's attitude to the curious triangle represented by Winston, Lloyd George and her father. When Winston left the Conservative Party for the first time and joined the Liberals, Asquith was very good and kind to him, a kind of father. Yet Winston sided with Lloyd George and it was because of their alliance that Asquith was pitched out of power in the middle of the war, and Lloyd George made Prime Minister in his place. What will Violet make of this, I wondered. She deals with Winston's role in tones of sorrow more than anger. He fell, she says, under Lloyd George's spell. Lloyd George educated him but he also corrupted him. Lloyd George taught him the radicalism which Winston because of his aristocratic background had never needed or wanted to learn. 'He [Winston] is full of the poor whom he has just discovered. He thinks he is called by providence – to do something for them.' But L.G. also seduced Winston. L.G. liked to beat the class-struggle drum. As early as 1908 Lady Violet was worried. 'He's come off on you,' she told Winston. 'You are talking like him instead of like yourself.' 'Somehow the words that rang true in his [L.G.'s] mouth rang false in Winston's. For the first time in my experience of him I felt that he was – quite unconsciously – wearing fancy dress, that he was not himself.'

Even after he had discovered the poor, and had sworn to help them, Winston wasn't really sound on them by Liberal standards, as witness his readiness to send the troops to smash the South Wales coal strike. It was clear that he preferred dreadnoughts to old-age pensions. His preparations for World War One were so enthusiastic that his Liberal colleagues were a bit embarrassed.

Winston, they said, seemed to like the idea of war. (He did.) However, Lady Violet went on giving Winston the benefit of the doubt. Then came another big shock to her confidence in him. As First Lord during World War One Winston went across to Antwerp. The port was being besieged by the Germans. The Belgians wanted to get out, and Winston went over to persuade them to hang on. To the consternation of the Cabinet, he cabled back to Asquith that he thought he (Winston) should chuck up the Admiralty and stay in Antwerp and take command of the forces in the field. Asquith took it rather well, really, merely refusing Winston's request – he was needed in the Admiralty – and noting 'Winston is an ex-lieutenant of Hussars, and would, if the proposal had been accepted, have been in command of two distinguished major-generals, not to mention brigadiers, colonels, etc.'

Lady Violet took a dimmer view. 'What amazed and shook me was the sense of proportion (or lack of it) revealed by Winston's choice ... it was hardly adult ... it was the choice of a romantic child.' I can assure her that in this respect Winston never quite grew up. He would have done the same kind of thing in World War Two if we had let him.

* * *

But worse was to come. Fisher, as First Lord, wrecked Winston's Dardanelles plans, and Winston knew it and bitterly complained. Fisher resigned. Winston left the Admiralty to fight in France. Three months later he was back in the House of Commons attacking the Government, talking of resigning his command, and urging the recall of Fisher to the Admiralty. 'Had I gone mad?' Lady Violet asked herself. 'Had Winston?' He shook everybody to the core. How unstable could you get? 'I saw ahead of me a parting of the ways between myself and Winston,' she writes on the last page of this magnificent book.

I hope I am alive to read Volume Two. We shall be told about the day that came 'when the paths that for so long had parted us suddenly met. And as they brought us face to face we knew we were once more side by side.'

Winston Churchill As I Knew Him, by Violet Bonham Carter. Collins and Eyre and Spottiswoode, 1965.

30
Mr. Macmillan's Early Political Life and Times

Mr. Macmillan is planning a very large literary venture, for this volume* of over 600 pages is to be the first of several volumes giving to the world his life story. It takes us only to 1939 – before he had attained office. He is therefore wise to open with a prologue in which he gives us a broad survey of his story. It is plain that this is more than a biography. It is not merely Macmillan, but his life and times.

The title, taken from his famous speech in South Africa, is well chosen, for he has lived through years which have seen greater changes in the history of the human race and in the way of life of the British people than ever before. Born in London in 1894, he has lived in six reigns and two world wars. His parents belonged to the middle well-to-do class and he was brought up in Chelsea on the fringe of the West End.

His forebears were Scots who had come to London and built up a most successful publishing business, but his mother was an American. Although 11 years older, I recall very well the kind of life which he lived in his early years, with a nurse and plenty of servants in a London of horses and carriages, steam trains and the more leisurely atmosphere of Victorian England. I recall the family visits to the seaside and the great public events such as the Jubilee (but mine was the golden and his the diamond) and the funeral of Queen Victoria. It is difficult for those born later to appreciate the atmosphere of Victorian England, when everything

*Harold Macmillan: *Winds of Change 1914–1939*, Macmillan, 1966.

seemed so secure and settled. Young Macmillan was well taught at home and proceeded in due course to the famous preparatory school of Summerfields at Oxford and then to Eton, where he was a scholar, and to Balliol, where he was an exhibitioner. All seemed set fair for a happy and prosperous life when the outbreak of the First World War brought everything to an end.

Aristocratic Entry

Macmillan, as soon as his health allowed it, joined up in Kitchener's Army but was transferred to the Grenadier Guards. He was one of the fortunate and brilliant young men of his generation to survive that war. In spite of being severely wounded at Loos and the Somme he was, thanks to the care of his mother and skilled medical treatment, restored to health – though the effects were lasting.

After the war Macmillan was uncertain what to do, but chance served him well. He was chosen to be an A.D.C. to the Duke of Devonshire, who had just been appointed Governor General of Canada. This, while widening his knowledge, also brought him his life's partner in Lady Dorothy Cavendish, and to a wide range of society not merely agreeable but qualifying him as a member of the aristocracy to lead the Conservative Party in the traditional way.

In the early twenties Macmillan worked in the publishing business which brought him into contact with many famous writers such as Hardy, Kipling, and H. G. Wells, but also allowed him to enjoy family gatherings at Chatsworth and elsewhere. In the disappearance of the great house since the Second World War one forgets that the old country house with its numbers of servants survived long after 1919. All this is very well described in this volume.

Macmillan, as a highly sensitive and intelligent young man, had fully shared the experience common to most of his generation of realizing the gulf between the classes, and understanding the outlook of the working class. As the years passed with the continuance of heavy unemployment and the failure of the Lloyd George Government to implement the promises of making a land fit for heroes, Macmillan began to wish to take action himself, and to seek a seat in Parliament. He was selected as candidate for

Stockton on Tees and though he just failed in 1923 was elected in 1924. He was, I think, fortunate in his constituency. A safe seat in the south might have lulled his interest in reform, but this Durham borough in a depressed area was a constant stimulus to independent action.

Dividing the Tories

I recall well his entrance to the House. At that time we divided the Tories into the Forty Thieves and the Y.M.C.A. Harold Macmillan was obviously a valuable recruit to the latter, the social reform Tories, men like J. W. Hills and Lord Henry Cavendish Bentinck, to whom we could look for sympathy and support.

During the years before 1931 Macmillan was the leader of a group of young Tories many of whom were destined to attain high office and who worked with great assiduity to try to get constructive ideas accepted by their party. These years included such events as the general strike, the Trade Disputes Bill, and various important measures. In thinking of Neville Chamberlain's failure as Prime Minister one is apt to forget his very considerable achievements as a social reformer, and how much he encouraged younger men in his party. The years of Macmillan's first Parliament are dealt with very fully – the story of Baldwin's administration with its constant unemployment and the quite considerable efforts to get rid of Baldwin, culminating in the Westminster by-election and his denunciation of the press lords, Beaverbrook and Rothermere.

Charitable to Labour

Foreign affairs were at this time going comparatively smoothly, with Austen Chamberlain at the Foreign Office and the various plans for the rehabilitation of Germany, so Macmillan concentrated on the home front, with other left-wing Tories. At the 1929 general election he lost his seat and did not regain it until 1931. He deals very charitably with the Labour Government, and naturally takes a much more favourable view of MacDonald and Snowden in 1931 than I should. He calls that chapter of his history the great divide. An interlude was a visit to Russia in 1932, when Macmillan seems to have been shown a great deal more than I was. He shows a wider comprehension of communism than would most of his party.

In the next Parliament Macmillan got more and more restive under the rule of the MacDonald-Baldwin coalition. He, like other young Conservatives, realized that the world was facing a new age and that constructive work was needed. In particular he had views of the need for planning. He seems to have become a close friend of Lord Allen of Hurtwood, from whom he got much inspiration. How we regarded Macmillan at that time is shown by a verse I wrote in a rude parody of 'The Red Flag' entitled 'The People's Flag is Palest Pink', at the time when Stafford Cripps was running the Popular Front:–

> *Look round the Liberal lancets blaze*
> *The cheerful mugwumps chant its praise*
> *In Hurtwood Hall its hymns are sung*
> *Macmillan thrills the surging throng.*

No one at that time would have dreamt that he would be preferred as a Conservative Prime Minister to the obedient Rab Butler, who was serving as Under-Secretary in the Foreign Office to John Simon.

Macmillan was reelected in the 1935 election and became increasingly hostile to the Conservative Government. He and younger Tories such as Rob Hudson, Eustace Percy, Bob Boothby, and Terence O'Connor worked out many suggestions, some of which were also embodied in articles and books – the most noteworthy being *The Middle Way*. Today most of these ideas have become commonplace and generally acceptable to Conservative opinion, and it is difficult for the present generation to realize how heretical they were at the time. With a huge majority the Chief Whip could afford to be tolerant, but eventually Macmillan wrote to Baldwin refusing the Whip – very drastic action for a Tory member.

Disastrous Quartet

After 1935 Macmillan's attention was turned to foreign affairs. I do not think there could have been a more disastrous quartet to be at the head of Great Britain during these fateful years than

MacDonald, Baldwin, Simon, and Chamberlain. Macmillan has some crisp remarks: for instance, he says of Simon 'His logical mind starting from false premises invariably arrived at the wrong conclusion'.

Needless to say when at last the critical decision was reached with the vote which brought the fall of Neville Chamberlain, Macmillan and his friends were found in the Labour lobby. During these years no office had ever been offered to Macmillan in spite of his obvious ability. He had to wait for the wartime government of Sir Winston Churchill, and we must wait for the next volume of his memoirs to learn his own account of his activities. This first volume is of great value, both for its account of the development of a future Prime Minister and for the account of a period in our national history from the pen of an acute participant in politics.

Epilogue

The District Commissioner in Downing Street

Attlee the penman was like Attlee the statesman – terse, telling and to the point. These admirable traits were more evident in his journalism than in his memoirs. Lady Violet Bonham-Carter, after a 1957 conversation with him at a Foyle's Lunch in the Dorchester, told her diary 'I like his flavour – rather like a caraway seed!'[1] This captures Attlee the book-reviewer to perfection. He could be very droll about Lady Vi, too, as we have seen in his reaction to her study of Winston Churchill. ('Amazing that her first book, at 78, should be so good. I wonder why she hasn't started before. Too busy talking, perhaps').

Violet was deeply touched by Clem's review, despite that barb, because '(1) He had clearly *enjoyed* reading the book enormously. (2) He had obviously felt a real *affection* and appreciation for W. (which W. *alas* did not reciprocate!) (3) He said it had given him a new apercu of my father [H H Asquith]'.[2] Clem on Winston is a golden thread running through this collection. And 'gold' is the right word. There was this classic Attlee collection lying waiting like gold if not quite in the streets but in the newspaper archives. And Frank Field has proved a connoisseur among prospectors.

We knew Attlee could produce stunning one-liners on political contemporaries. My favourite is to be found in the Granada Television interview recorded in 1965, two years before his death:

'Queer bird, Halifax. Very humorous, all hunting and Holy Communion'.[3]

Perfection. But Frank Field has shown us by compiling this

175

collection that as a biographical miniaturist Attlee was truly top flight.

His gift is all the more appealing because he was deeply averse to touching-up or exaggerating his own autobiography. My favourite passage in the Granada transcript is when the hapless interviewer tries to draw out the old man on the subject of political destiny:

Interviewer: What were your emotions at becoming Prime Minister?
Attlee: Just to know that there were jobs that were to be done.
Interviewer: You didn't feel that destiny had overtaken you?
Attlee: No. I had not much idea about destiny.
Interviewer: Have you ever felt in any way, Lord Attlee, as being, in fact as you are, a man of destiny? Have you ever felt this kind of emotion which Winston Churchill has written about so much?
Attlee: No, you see I didn't regard myself as a potential hero.[4]

Humility convincingly and, in terms of the interviewer, lethally deployed.

Attlee's shyness and modesty did not convert into indecision or lack of self-confidence, however. In Frank Field's collection the articles and reviews which exhibit the surest touch are those devoted to statecraft and premiership. When it came to the proper and effective conduct of Cabinet government, 'little Clem' as the bulk-carrier in the Foreign Office, Ernie Bevin, liked to call him,[5] rather cornered the market in memorable quips. 'Democracy', he told a group of Oxford undergraduates in 1957, 'means government by discussion, but it is only effective if you can stop people talking.'[6]

Essays 18 and 19 in this volume are gems of the genre – and, sadly, the prolix Harold Wilson did not heed Attlee's advice on how to run a Cabinet which the *Observer* ran on the Sunday after the 1964 general election.

Reading both Frank Field's commentary and Attlee's cuttings library left me saddened. First it is impossible to imagine such a figure as terse 'little Clem' rising to the top in today's sound-

bitten, celebrity politics. He probably wouldn't get selected for a
losable seat let alone a winnable one. Just imagine Attlee replying
to questions at a selection conference:

'Yes'
'No'
'Quite'
'Perhaps'
'Needs watching'

I remain convinced that if, by some benign fluke, a decent,
modest, understated figure *did* reach the top of a party today,
great political advantage would accrue to him or her. And how
we would love watching him or her on *Newsnight* or listening to
him or her on the *Today* programme.

We know how Attlee would have sounded. Here he is causing
havoc with a series of staccato replies to a newsreel interviewer in
the opening days of the 1951 general election campaign:

Interviewer:	Tell us something on how you view the election prospects.
Attlee:	Oh, we shall go in with a good fight. Very good. Very good chance of winning if we go in competently. We always do.
Interviewer:	On what will Labour take its stand?
Attlee:	Well, that's what we shall be announcing shortly.
Interviewer:	What are your immediate plans Mr Attlee?
Attlee:	My immediate plans are to go down to a committee to decide on just that thing as soon as I can get away from here.
Interviewer:	Is there anything else you'd like to say about the coming election?
Attlee:	No.[7]

Attlee was a stranger to media training and all the more effective
for it.

For British politics generally he set a gold standard for the
proper and fruitful conduct of Cabinet government. For centre-
left politicians he set an ethical gold standard too. He always, for
me, carried the imprint of his school – the Imperial Service
College at Haileybury. For Attlee was four-square in the best of

the imperial tradition – decent, high-minded and steeped and marinated in a certain idea of duty. His territory, however, was not some vast swathe of Kenya. It was 1940s and early 1950s Britain when we oscillated between housing an imperial warrior and a district commissioner in No. 10. The social and political compost that made Winston and Clem is long gone. But those with an ear to hear and a political sensibility to see can, as Frank Field has done, discover real and usable treasure from those six years when brevity and understatement prevailed in the Cabinet Room. Clem Attlee was no destiny politician, no primary colours premier. But he was an ace among prime ministers.

Peter Hennessy, FBA
Attlee Professor of Contemporary British History
Queen Mary
University of London.

---

[1] Mark Pottle (ed), *Daring to Hope: The Diaries and Letters of Violet Bonham-Carter, 1946–1969* (Weidenfeld, 2000), p. 192, diary entry for 6 December 1957

[2] ibid, p. 301, diary entry for 6 April 1965

[3] *Clem Attlee: The Granada Historical Records Interview*, (Panther Record, 1967), p. 20

[4] ibid, p. 29

[5] Douglas Jay, *Change and Fortune: A Political Record*, (Hutchinson, 1980), p. 135

[6] 'Duty of ruthless sacking: "Stop Cabinet Talking"', *The Times*, 15 June 1957

[7] Quoted in Peter Hennessy, *The Prime Minister: The Office and Its Holders since 1945*, (Penguin, 2001), p. 170

Index